THE
COMPLETE
SPORTS
DICTIONARY

• • • • • • • • • • • • • • • • •

THE COMPLETE SPORTS DICTIONARY

....

GEORGE SULLIVAN

SCHOLASTIC INC.
New York Toronto London Auckland Sydney

No part of this publication may be reproduced in whole or in part, or stored in a retrieval system, or transmitted in any form or by any means, electronic, mechanical, photocopying, recording, or otherwise, without written permission of the publisher. For information regarding permission, write to Scholastic Inc., 730 Broadway, New York, NY 10003.

ISBN 0-590-40411-3

12 11 10 9 8 7 6 5 4 3 2 1   10   3 4 5 6 7 8/9

THE
COMPLETE
SPORTS
DICTIONARY

....

Introduction

What is a dunk? What is a pick?

What is the difference between a double foul and a double fault?

How do you figure a baseball player's batting average?

These and countless other questions are answered in *The Complete Sports Dictionary*, the first book of its kind for young readers. It defines hundreds of words and terms common to some 50 different sports.

The book covers not only baseball, basketball, soccer, football, and other popular team sports, but also recreational activities such as tennis, swimming, and golf. Even in-line skating is included.

Whether you're a third baseman or a point guard, or simply get your enjoyment from sports as a spectator, this book is for you. Increasing your knowledge of the sports that interest you makes them easier to understand, follow — and enjoy. Have fun!

A

ace: *Tennis:* A serve which one's opponent fails to return. *Golf:* A hole in one.

ad court, advantage court: *Tennis:* The service court on the receiver's left.

advantage: *Tennis:* The point scored immediately after deuce. The player winning the advantage point wins the game. Should the opposing player win the advantage point, the score becomes deuce again. See deuce.

air ball: *Basketball:* A shot that completely misses the backboard and the rim.

all-America: A member of a team of players voted best in the United States. All-Americas can be either high school or college athletes.

alley: *Bowling:* The smooth, level surface, made entirely of wood, upon which the ball is rolled. It is 60 feet in length and approximately 41 inches in width. *Baseball:* The area between two outfielders. *Tennis:* The narrow strip of court that borders each of the singles sidelines. The alleys are used only in doubles.

all-pro: A professional player named as the best in his position. All-pro teams are common to football and basketball.

all-star: A player named to a team composed of outstanding players.

All-Star Game: A baseball contest held annually since 1933 between all-star teams representing the National League and American League. All-Star Games are also common to professional basketball and ice hockey.

Alpine: *Skiing:* Downhill skiing or downhill competition.

also-ran: A competitor who is defeated in a race.

amateur: An athlete who has never competed for money.

Amateur Athletic Union (AAU): An association of amateur athletic clubs and organizations; the governing body for amateur track and field, basketball, boxing, gymnastics, handball, swimming, water polo, wrestling, weight lifting, judo, and horseshoe pitching.

American Bowling Congress (ABC): The official rule-making body of tenpin bowling.

American Junior Bowling Congress (AJBC): The governing body of bowling for boys and girls in the United States.

American League (AL): An association of teams in professional baseball; one of baseball's two major leagues. The American League champion meets the National League champion in the World Series each fall.

American Softball Association (ASA): The governing body of amateur softball in the United States.

American Youth Soccer Organization (AYSO): An independent organization of amateur teams of boys and girls that provides competition on a state, regional, and national basis.

America's Cup: A trophy originally won by the yacht *America* in 1851 off the Isle of Wight in England. Now, the trophy that is awarded to the winner of a series of international races between a selected American yacht and a foreign challenger.

anchor man: A member of a team, heavily depended upon, who is the last to perform in a relay race, as in track or swimming. The anchor man in bowling is the last to perform for his team.

apprentice jockey: A jockey who is learning the trade and is thus entitled to special consideration. A horse ridden by an apprentice is given a reduction in the weight it must carry, the amount ranging from three to five pounds.

approach: *Bowling:* The area where the bowler takes his stance and strides forward to release the ball. Also called the runway.

approach shot: *Golf:* Any stroke made following the drive from the tee with which one seeks to get the ball to the putting green.

aquaplane: A flat board, five to six feet in length, on which one rides on a standing position while it is being pulled over the water by a speedboat.

3

arabesque: A body position common to gymnastics and figure skating (and ballet) in which the performer stands on one leg, leans forward from the waist, and extends the other leg backward with a straight knee.

archer: Someone skilled in the use of a bow and arrow.

archery: The sport of shooting with a bow and arrow.

archery golf: A game played on a golf course in which bows, arrows, and targets substitute for clubs, balls, and holes. Scoring is the same as in golf, with each shot counting as a stroke.

arm wrestling: A sport in which two opponents sit face to face across a table and grip one another's hands, placing the elbows on the table surface. The object is to then force each other's arm to the table.

armstand dive: Any of a number of dives that begin with the diver in a handstand position at the end of the platform and facing toward it.

arrow: A straight, thin shaft shot from a bow made of wood, metal, or fiberglass. It has a pointed tip at one end and feathers at the other to stabilize its flight.

assist: *Baseball, Softball:* A throw made to a teammate who, in turn, makes a putout. *Basketball, Soccer:* A pass to a teammate who immediately scores. *Ice Hockey:* A play involving the handling of the puck that leads to a teammate's scoring.

4

Association for Intercollegiate Athletics for Women (AIAW): The governing body of women's college sports.

Astroturf: A type of synthetic surface used in place of grass.

at bat: *Baseball, Softball:* An official turn as a batter. There are occasions when a batter is not charged with a time at bat: when he receives a base on balls, when he is hit by a pitched ball, when he is interfered with by the catcher, and when he sacrifices.

attacking zone: *Ice Hockey:* The zone in which the opponent's goal is located and which extends from the goal line to the nearest blue line. One team's attacking zone is the other team's defensive zone. See defensive zone, neutral zone.

audible: *Football:* A play called by the quarterback at the line of scrimmage that changes the play called in the huddle. Also called an automatic.

automatic: *Football:* See audible.

B

baby split: *Bowling:* The 2-7 or 3-10 split.

back: *Football:* A member of the offensive backfield: the quarterback or either of the two running backs; also, a member of the defensive backfield: either of the two safeties or two cornerbacks. *Soccer:* The right and left fullback and the right, left, and center half-backs. *Volleyball:* Any of the three players positioned in the second row at the time the ball is served.

backboard: *Basketball:* The elevated board from which the basket projects. It can be rectangular (measuring four feet by six feet) or fan-shaped (54 inches wide).

back check: *Ice Hockey:* To skate back toward one's own goal while defending against an opposing player who is attacking.

backcourt: *Basketball:* That half of the court containing the basket a team is defending.

backcourt foul: *Basketball:* A foul against a team that is within that half of the court containing the basket it is defending.

backcourt violation: *Basketball:* A violation that results from a team's failure to bring the ball from its backcourt to its forecourt within 10 seconds after gaining possession.

back dive: See backward dive.

backdoor play: *Basketball:* An offensive play in which a player darts away from his defender and toward the baseline, then cuts for the basket and a pass.

backfield: *Football:* Offensive and defensive players who line up behind the linemen. (Exclusive of linebackers on defense.)

backhand: In tennis and other racket sports, a stroke made on the left side of the body by a right-handed player, on the right by a left-handed one.

back judge: *Football:* A football official who watches for clips and pass interference, and rules on field goals and where the ball goes out of bounds.

back nine: *Golf:* The last nine holes on an 18-hole course.

backspin: In various racket sports, spin applied by hitting the ball with a downward motion of the racket. *Billiards, Pocket Billiards:* Spin that causes the cue ball to stop or move backward, toward the shooter, after hitting the object ball.

backstretch: *Racing:* On an oval race track, the straight section opposite the homestretch and the finish line.

backstroke: *Swimming:* A swimming stroke executed with the swimmer on his back, using a frog kick and stroking the arms alternately.

back-up ball: *Bowling:* A bowled ball that breaks in the direction opposite of what is normal; for a right-handed bowler, a ball that breaks to the right.

backward dive: *Diving:* A dive in which the diver first stands on the board facing away from the water, then jumps up and rotates backward, so as to enter the water headfirst.

backward roll: *Gymnastics:* A stunt in which the body rolls over backward, heels over head; a backward somersault.

badminton: A game in which a shuttlecock is hit back and forth over a high, narrow net by means of a light long-handled racket.

bag: *Baseball, Softball:* A base.

bail out: *Baseball, Softball:* To draw back from the plate in order to avoid being hit by a pitched ball.

bait: *Fishing:* Worms, insects, bait fish, corn kernels, balls of dough, or other food that is attached to a hook in an attempt to catch fish.

bait casting: *Fishing:* A type of fishing using bait or an artificial lure and a casting rod. See fly casting.

balance beam: *Gymnastics:* A wooden beam, approximately 16 feet (five meters) in length and four inches (10 centimeters) in width, and which is mounted on supports that place it about four feet (120 centimeters) above the floor. Various tumbling and dance movements are performed on the beam.

balanced line: *Football:* A formation in which there are an equal number of linemen on either side of the center.

balk: *Baseball:* An incomplete or misleading motion by the pitcher with one or more runners on base. To penalize the pitcher, the runners are permitted to advance one base.

ball boy; ball girl: An individual who retrieves balls for the players in a tennis match, or retrieves foul balls and brings new balls to the umpire during a baseball game.

ball hawk: *Basketball:* An aggressive defensive player who dives for and recovers loose balls, blocks passes and shots, and makes steals and interceptions.

Baltimore chop: *Baseball:* A batted ball that strikes home plate or the ground near home plate to rebound high into the air. The batter can often beat out a Baltimore chop for a base hit.

banana blade: *Ice Hockey:* A stick blade with a bigger than normal curve.

bank: To shoot a ball so that it rebounds from a wall, backboard, or cushion.

barbell: A bar with adjustable disc-shaped weights at each end, used for exercise or in the sport of weight lifting.

bareback riding: *Rodeo:* An event in which contestants seek to ride a bucking horse for a period of eight seconds. The horse has no saddle. Riders hold onto a handle attached to a strap around the horse's midsection.

base: *Baseball, Softball:* One of the three white canvas bags, 15 inches square, placed at the corners of the infield. Home plate is also considered a base. The bases must be touched or occupied in sequence in order for the base runner to score a run.

baseball: A game played with a bat and ball by two teams of nine players each on a field with bases arranged in a 90-foot square. The team having the most runs at the end of a nine-inning game is the winner. For a run to score, an offensive player must touch each base in sequence in a counterclockwise direction. Teams take turns playing on offense and defense. A pitcher, positioned 60 feet, six inches, away from the batter, pitches to the catcher. The batter, standing beside home plate, attempts to hit the ball between fielders so he can run to one or more of the bases without being put out. A team continues to bat until three men have been put out.

baseball grip: *Golf:* A method of gripping the club in which the two hands grasp it in the same manner a baseball bat is gripped by a batter, that is, without any overlapping or interlocking of the fingers. See Vardon grip, interlocking grip.

base hit: *Baseball, Softball:* A ball struck into fair territory which allows the batter to reach first base safely, provided an error, force out, or fielder's choice does not take place on the play.

baseline: *Baseball:* A path between bases, bounded by imaginary lines; a basepath. *Basketball:* Each of the court's end lines. *Tennis, Volleyball:* Each of the lines at the opposing back ends of the court and behind which a player must stand when serving.

baseline game: *Tennis:* A style of play in which one stays behind or near the baseline, relying on a succession of ground strokes.

base on balls: *Baseball, Softball:* The right of the batter to advance to first base after receiving four pitches outside the strike zone (which he did not swing at). Also called a walk or pass.

basepath: See baseline.

base runner: *Baseball, Softball:* A player who has reached base safely or is attempting to reach base.

basket: *Basketball:* Either of the two goals, each consisting of a metal hoop, 18 inches in diameter, from which a cord net hangs. Also, a field goal. *Skiing:* A ring fixed to the ski pole

10

at a point about four to six inches from the tip that serves to keep the pole from sinking too deeply into the snow.

basketball: A game played on a rectangular court by two teams of five players each, the object of which is to toss the ball through an elevated goal which consists of a metal rim 18 inches in diameter mounted 10 feet above the floor on a wood, metal, or glass backboard.

basket catch: *Baseball, Softball:* A catch of a fly ball at waist level, the glove and the bare hand cradling the ball.

bat: *Baseball, Softball:* The rounded wooden or metal stick used by the batter to hit the ball. Also, to take a turn at the plate, attempting to hit a pitched ball.

bat boy; bat girl: *Baseball, Softball:* An individual who takes care of players' equipment, chiefly bats, always retrieving the bat from home plate after a batter has become a base runner.

baton: *Track:* The hollow stick of wood, metal, or plastic, approximately 12 inches in length, that is carried by each runner in a relay race. The baton is passed to the runner who is to run the next leg of the race within a designated exchange zone.

batter: *Baseball, Softball:* The player whose turn it is to bat.

batter's box: *Baseball:* Either of the two rectangles, four feet by six feet in size, marked on the field on either side of and six inches from home plate. The batter must stand within one of the boxes when taking a turn at the plate.

battery: *Baseball, Softball:* The pitcher and the catcher.

batting average: *Baseball, Softball:* A statistic used to indicate a batter's effectiveness, and obtained by dividing the number of base hits by the number of official times at bat, and carrying out the result to three decimal places. Thus, a player with 176 hits in 560 times at bat has a batting average of .314.

batting order: *Baseball, Softball:* The sequence in which players take their turns at bat.

bean: *Baseball:* To hit the batter on the head with a pitch.

beanball: *Baseball:* A pitch that hits the batter on the head, or one that is thrown close to his head to frighten him.

beat board: *Gymnastics:* A rectangular springboard, about 30 inches long, used to gain upward motion in vaulting, tumbling, and mounting the beam. Also called a Reuther board.

beat out: *Baseball, Softball:* To reach first base safely after hitting a weak grounder to the infield.

bed: *Billiards, Pocket Billiards:* The flat surface of the table, frequently made of slate.

bedpost: *Bowling:* A split in which the 7 and 10 pins are left standing.

behind: *Baseball, Softball:* A situation in which the count is to the pitcher's disadvantage, that is, when the pitcher has thrown more balls than strikes.

bell lap: *Track, Cycling:* The last lap of a race.

bench: To remove a player from a game.

bench jockey: A player who rides (heckles) opposition players from the bench or dugout.

bench press: *Weight Lifting:* A lift performed while lying on one's back on a bench. The lifter pushes up the barbell from his chest to arm's length, then lowers it to the chest again.

bicycle kick: An exercise performed while lying on one's back with the hips and legs in the air, the hips supported by the hands. The legs move up and down, as if pedaling a bicycle.

big four: *Bowling:* A split in which the 4, 6, 7, and 10 pins are left standing.

big man: The center on a basketball team.

billiards: Any of several games played on a rectangular, cloth-covered, pocketless table with raised cushioned edges, in which a long slender cue is used to hit three small hard balls against one another or against the cushions.

binding: *Skiing:* The device by which the ski is fastened to the boot.

bird: *Badminton:* See shuttlecock. *Skeet, Trapshooting:* See clay pigeon.

birdcage: *Football:* The face mask worn by linemen that features extra horizontal and vertical bars.

birdie: *Golf:* One stroke less than par for a hole.

bit: *Horseback Riding:* The metal mouthpiece of the horse's bridle.

black belt: An award given to one who has earned a rating of expert in judo or karate.

black flag: *Auto Racing:* The solid black flag that serves to signal a driver to come into the pit.

blackout: To prohibit the telecasting of a sports event in a specific area.

blade: *Skating:* The hollow-edged length of steel mounted to the skate bottom upon which the skater travels.

blank: *Baseball:* To hold an opposing team scoreless.

bleachers: An unroofed outdoor grandstand for seating spectators, usually in baseball.

blind: A shelter for concealing hunters.

blinders: *Horse Racing:* See blinkers.

blind pass: A pass made by a player to a teammate without looking at the teammate.

blind side: The side away from which a player is looking.

blinkers: *Horse Racing:* Eye shades with which nervous horses are sometimes fitted.

blitz: *Football:* The headlong charge into the offensive backfield by one or more linebackers and defensive backs. The object of a blitz is to deck the quarterback, or at least interfere with his attempt to pass. Also called red dog.

block: *Football:* To interfere with or otherwise prevent the movement of an opposing defensive player. Also, to clear opposing players out of the path of the ballcarrier.

blooper: *Baseball, Softball:* A safely hit fly ball that goes just beyond the infield.

blow: See error (bowling).

blue flag: *Auto Racing:* The solid blue flag used to signal a driver to give way to a faster vehicle that is attempting to pass.

blue line: *Ice Hockey:* Either of two blue lines, each one foot wide, that extend the width of the rink at a distance of 60 feet from the goal lines, and which serve to divide the rink into zones.

blunt: *Archery:* An arrow with a flattened tip used in hunting small game.

boards: *Ice Hockey:* The wooden barrier, three to four feet in height, that surrounds the rink. *Basketball:* The backboards.

bob and weave: *Boxing:* To move one's upper body from side to side and forward and back in an effort to avoid an opponent's punches.

bobber: *Fishing:* See float.

bobsled: A long, sturdy racing sled with two pairs of double runners, one pair mounted behind the other. The bobsled is steered by a mechanism that controls the front runners.

body check: *Ice Hockey:* To use one's upper body to slow or stop an opponent.

body surf: To ride a wave without a surfboard, on one's chest and belly.

bogey: *Golf:* A score of one stroke over par on a hole.

bomb: *Football:* A very long forward pass that results in a touchdown.

bomb squad: See special team.

bonus free throw: *Basketball:* The additional free throw awarded to a player who has been fouled when the opposing team has exceeded the number of team fouls permitted during a period of play. In high school competition, a bonus free throw is awarded after five team fouls have been committed in a period. In pro basketball, the bonus free throw is awarded after four team fouls in a quarter.

bonus situation: *Basketball:* The situation that applies when a team has exceeded the number of team fouls permitted for a period.

boom: *Sailing:* The horizontal pole, attached to the mast at one end, and to which the foot of the sail is fastened.

boot: *Skiing:* The heavy, rigid, ankle-length covering to which the binding is secured. *Harness Racing:* A protective covering for a horse's lower leg. *Baseball:* An error made in attempting to field a ground ball.

bootleg: *Football:* An offensive play in which the quarterback conceals the ball at his hip, and hurries to one side to run or pass.

bottom time: In underwater diving, the amount of time a diver has spent beneath the surface.

bounce pass: *Basketball:* A pass made by rebounding the ball from the floor to the receiver.

bow: *Archery:* A strip of curved elastic wood or plastic with a hand grip in the middle and tapered on both ends, that is strung from end to end and is used to launch arrows.

bow arm: *Archery:* The arm that supports the bow when shooting.

bow fishing: The sport of catching fish, or attempting to catch them, with a bow and special arrows.

bow hand: *Archery:* The hand that holds the bow.

bow hunting: The sport of pursuing game or wild animals with a bow and arrow.

bowl game: A post-season football game that matches specially invited teams.

bowling: Any of several games played by rolling a ball down a wooden alley in order to knock down a triangular group of pins. Bowling can also refer to lawn bowling.

bowling average: A statistic that indicates one's average bowling score for a specific period — a series of three games, a week, or a season. It is found by dividing the total number of pins for which a bowler has received credit, by the number of games bowled. Thus, a bowler credited with 1,848 pins in 12 games would have a 154 average.

bowling pin: One of a triangular group of 10 pins at which the ball is aimed in various bowling games.

bowman: Someone skilled in the use of a bow and arrow; an archer.

bowsight: *Archery:* An aiming device attached to the bow.

box: *Bowling:* A square on the score sheet; a frame.

boxing: The sport of fighting with the fists.

box out: *Basketball:* To position oneself between an opposing player and the basket, so as to block the opponent from the ball as it rebounds from the backboard or the basket.

boxscore: A printed summary of a game giving the names of the players and statistical information regarding the performance of each. Boxscores are common to baseball and basketball.

break: *Baseball, Softball:* To curve a ball near or over the plate. *Billiards, Pocket Billiards:* The opening shot of a game or rack. *Basketball:* See fast break. *Tennis:* See service break.

break out: *Ice Hockey:* The instance of a team bringing the puck out from behind its goal and starting up the ice.

break point: *Tennis:* A situation in which the receiving player or side has the opportunity to break an opponent's serve by winning the next point. The score is usually love-40, 15-40, or 30-40 at the time.

break shot: *Billiards, Pocket Billiards:* The opening shot of a game or match.

breast stroke: *Swimming:* A stroke in which the swimmer lies facedown in the water and extends the arms in front of the head, then sweeps them back together under the surface of the water while executing a frog kick.

bridge: *Billiards, Pocket Billiards:* The support formed by the left hand (of right-handed players) for guiding the cue when making a shot.

bridle: *Horseback Riding:* The harness that fits over a horse's head, consisting of a bit, headstall, and reins, and which is used to control and guide the animal.

broadhead: *Archery:* An arrow with a flat steel blade used in hunting.

broad jump: See long jump.

bronc, bronco: A pony of the western United States, often wild or partly tamed.

bronco-buster: A cowboy who trains broncos to the saddle.

bronze medal: In the Olympic games and other sports competition, the bronze or bronze-colored medal awarded for a third-place finish.

Brooklyn: *Bowling:* A hit on the left side of the headpin (for a right-handed bowler). Also called a Jersey.

broom ball: *Bowling:* See sweeper.

brush back: *Baseball, Softball:* To attempt to move a batter away from the plate by pitching the ball high and inside.

bucket: *Bowling:* A spare in which the 2, 4, 5, and 8 pins are left standing.

buddy breathing: *Scuba Diving:* The sharing of one tank of air by two divers. The mouthpiece is passed back and forth, each diver taking only one or two breaths at a time.

buddy line: *Scuba Diving:* A line that is tied to two divers to prevent them from becoming separated.

buddy system: In swimming and underwater diving, a system in which paired individuals are made responsible for one another's safety.

bulldog: *Rodeo:* To wrestle a steer to the ground by seizing its horns and twisting its neck until the animal falls.

bullpen: *Baseball:* The area where relief pitchers warm up during a game.

bull's-eye: The center of a target.

bumper pool: A type of pool played on a small, two-hole table in which cushioned pegs dot the playing surface.

bunker: *Golf:* A sand trap or other obstacle on the course.

bunny hop: *Figure Skating:* A jump in which the skater vaults into the air from one skate, touches down briefly on the toe picks of the other skate, and lands on the blade of the starting skate.

bunt: *Baseball, Softball:* A ball that is batted by holding the bat almost motionless, causing the ball to roll slowly in front of the infielders.

bush league: A baseball minor league. Also, anything second rate in character or quality.

butterfly, butterfly stroke: *Swimming:* A variation of the breast stroke in which both arms are pulled upward out of the water and brought forward together. This arm action is combined with an up-and-down kick of both feet.

buttonhook: *Football:* A pass route in which the receiver heads straight downfield, then ab-

ruptly turns back toward the line of scrimmage.

bye: The position of an individual who draws no
opponent for a round in a tournament, and is
thus able to advance to the next round without
playing. Byes are common to tennis and golf.

C

cactus league: *Baseball:* The exhibition game
competition in spring training among teams
that train in the southwestern United States.

caddie: *Golf:* One who assists by carrying a player's clubs.

cager: A basketball player.

calf roping: *Rodeo:* An event in which a mounted
cowboy is required to rope a calf from horseback, then dismount, throw the calf, and tie
any three of the animal's legs.

calisthenics: Simple physical exercises that involve bending, twisting, swinging, kicking, and
jumping movements. They include such exercises as the push-up, sit-up, bicycle kick, and
chin-up.

camber: *Skiing:* The slightly arched surface of
the ski.

Canadian football: A game similar to American
football, but with certain exceptions: The field
is 110 yards in length vs. 100 yards in American

football. There are 12 players on a team instead of 11, and a team is allowed only three downs to advance the ball 10 yards, not four downs.

Canadian Football League (CFL): An association of professional football clubs representing many of the principal cities of Canada.

candlepins: A game of bowling common to certain sections of the United States, chiefly New England, in which slender candle-shaped pins, each 15 inches in height, are used. The alley is the same as in tenpin bowling. The ball is five inches in diameter. A game consists of 10 frames, with three balls to a frame.

canter: A gait slower than a gallop but faster than a trot.

captain: A member of a team who represents the team as a spokesman and who may be assigned to make certain decisions for the team. A captain is usually elected by his fellow players, but sometimes club officials appoint the player who is to serve.

carom: *Billiards, Pocket Billiards:* The action of the cue ball when it glances off one object ball into another. Also, in such games as straight rail billiards, a carom is a score or a count.

cartwheel: *Gymnastics:* A handspring in which the body turns over sideways.

cast: *Gymnastics:* In stunts on the parallel bars, to push or thrust the body away from the point of support.

casting: *Fishing:* Throwing a baited hook or line into the water.

casting rod: *Fishing:* A thin, lightweight rod, four to six feet in length, with a reel mounted near the handle, used for casting bait or lures.

catamaran: A boat with two parallel hulls.

catcher: *Baseball, Softball:* The player whose position is behind home plate and who signals for and receives the pitches.

catching glove: *Ice Hockey:* The glove that resembles a baseball first baseman's mitt that is worn by the goalkeeper and used to catch the puck on shots fired at the goal.

catgut: A tough, thin cord from the dried intestines of certain animals, used for stringing tennis rackets.

center: *Basketball:* The member of the team who usually plays the pivot and takes part in the center jump. *Football:* The member of the offensive team who plays in the middle of the line and snaps the ball back between his legs to the quarterback, kicker, or holder.

centerboard: *Sailing:* A flat board or metal blade that can be lowered through the bottom of a small boat to prevent drifting and increase stability.

center circle: *Basketball:* The four-foot circle in the center of the court from which the tip-off is made. *Soccer:* The 20-yard circle in the middle of the field from which the kickoff is made.

center field: *Baseball, Softball:* The outfield area between right field and left field.

center fielder: *Baseball, Softball:* The player who plays center field.

center halfback: *Soccer:* A primarily defensive player who covers the midfield area and normally guards the opposing center forward.

center ice: The neutral zone of an ice hockey rink.

center jump: *Basketball:* The jump that takes place between opposing centers at the center of the court at the beginning of a period.

center mark: *Tennis:* The mark on the baseline that divides it into equal halves and helps the server in taking his or her position.

center service line: *Tennis:* The line that divides the front part of the court into two service courts.

cesta: *Jai Alai:* The long curved wicker basket that is strapped to the lower arm and used to throw and catch the ball.

chain crew: *Football:* The group of three assistants to the officials who handle the first-down measuring chain and the down box, keeping track of the ball on each series of downs.

chair lift: The power-driven chair assembly suspended from an overhead cable that is used in transporting skiers up the slopes.

chance: *Baseball, Softball:* Any opportunity to catch or field a batted ball.

change-over: In various net games, the exchange of sides of the court with one's opponent. Players change courts to equalize conditions of lighting, wind, and background. In tennis, a change-over occurs whenever the game score total is an odd number, such as 1-0, 3-2, or 5-4. In table tennis and volleyball, courts are changed after each game.

change-up, change of pace: *Baseball, Softball:* A slow pitch thrown with the same motion as the pitcher's fastball, and meant to deceive the batter. Also called a letup.

charging: *Ice Hockey:* A foul that results when a player runs or jumps into an opponent after taking two or more steps. *Basketball:* A personal foul that results when a player with the ball, or a player who just has taken a shot or passed, runs into a defensive player. *Soccer:* A foul that results when a player rushes at an opponent from behind, or in a violent or dangerous manner.

cheap shot: An act of deliberate violence against an opponent, and one that is committed when the opponent is not expecting it and is not able to defend himself.

check: *Ice Hockey:* Any means by which a player causes an opponent to lose the puck or prevents him from receiving it.

checkered flag: *Auto Racing:* The flag bearing black and white squares used at the finish of a race to signal to a driver that he has won and to the other contestants that the race is over.

check off: *Football:* To change a play at the line of scrimmage by calling an audible.

chest protector: *Baseball:* A padded or inflated cushion-like shield worn by the catcher and umpire especially to guard against foul tips.

chin-up: An exercise in which one pulls the body up with the arms while grasping a horizontal bar until the chin is level with the bar.

chip shot: *Golf:* A short and usually low approach shot. Also called a pitch-and-run.

choke, choke up: To fail to perform up to one's ability in a critical situation because of nervous tension. Also, to grip a bat, racket, or club near the hitting surface; to shorten one's grip.

Christmas tree: *Bowling:* A split in which the 3, 7, and 10 pins are left standing. *Drag Racing:* A set of colored lights arranged in two columns on a vertical pole at the starting line and which are used for signaling competitors in starting a race.

chukker: *Polo:* One of the periods of play, lasting 7½ minutes. A game normally consists of six chukkers.

chum: *Fishing:* Bait that usually consists of oily fish ground or chopped up and thrown into the water to attract fish.

chumming: *Fishing:* Attracting fish by throwing out chum from the shore or a boat. Once the fish begin to appear, baited hooks are put into the water. Chumming is illegal in many states.

circle eight: *Figure Skating:* A skating figure that consists of two adjacent circles, each skated and completed from a specific starting point. The two circles form the figure 8.

circus catch: Any catch that is characterized by a sensational element, such as diving and rolling on the ground.

claiming race: *Horse Racing:* A race in which each horse entered is available for purchase at a price fixed before the race.

clay court: *Tennis:* A court with a clay surface or a fine-grained synthetic surface that resembles clay.

clay pigeon: *Skeet, Trapshooting:* A thin clay disk, slightly smaller than a saucer, thrown as a flying target. Also called a bird.

clean and jerk: *Weight Lifting:* A lift in which one lifts the weight from the floor to shoulder level in one continuous motion, then, on a signal from the referee, thrusts the weight overhead, fully extending the arms.

clean game: *Bowling:* A game with either a strike or spare in every frame.

clean-up batter: *Baseball, Softball:* The hitter that bats fourth in a team's batting order.

clear: *Badminton:* A shot that is hit high and deep into the opponent's court.

clearing kick: *Soccer:* Any kick that sends the ball away from one's goal and toward the opposite end of the field.

cleat: A rubber, plastic, or metal projection attached to the underside of a shoe to prevent slipping.

cliff-hanger: A game or other event that is so closely contested that its outcome is uncertain until the very end.

clinch: To win a championship before the end of the season by building a lead so great that it cannot be overcome by an opponent. *Boxing:* To hold an opponent with one or both arms so as to prevent or hinder his punches.

clip: *Football:* To block an opponent from behind, usually across the back of the legs. Clipping is illegal and results in a 15-yard penalty.

clock: To record the time or speed of a runner or a racehorse over a measured course with a stopwatch or electronic timer.

clocker: A person who times racehorses during their workouts.

closed stance: *Baseball, Softball:* A batter's position when awaiting the pitch in which the front foot is closer to the plate than the rear foot.

clothesline: *Football:* To strike an opponent, often a pass receiver breaking downfield, across the face or neck with an extended forearm. Clotheslining is illegal.

coach: A person who trains athletes or athletic teams. Coaching duties and responsibilities vary widely from sport to sport. In gymnastics and figure skating, the coach works closely with each pupil to perfect form and style. In team sports such as basketball and football, the coach is more concerned with developing offensive and defensive tactics and strategy.

coach's box: *Baseball, Softball:* Each of two rectangular areas just outside the baselines near first and third bases within which the coaches must remain when the ball is in play.

cock feather: *Archery:* The feather that is at right angles to the bow when the arrow is drawn.

Usually a different color than the other two feathers, it helps in locating the position of the notch at the arrow end.

cockfighting: A sport, now illegal, in which specially trained gamecocks, often with metal spurs, fight each other until one is disabled or killed.

cockpit: *Auto Racing:* The space in which the driver sits in a racing car. *Boating:* The open area of a small boat, lower than the rest of the deck, from which the boat is steered.

coin toss: *Football:* The ceremony before a game in which a coin is flipped to decide which team will receive the kickoff. The team that loses the toss is permitted to designate which goal it wishes to defend.

collapse, collapsing defense: *Basketball:* See sag, sagging.

colt: A young male horse.

combination: *Boxing:* A series of punches delivered in rapid succession.

combination shot: *Billiards, Pocket Billiards:* A shot in which the cue ball causes two or more balls to hit each other in sequence.

complete game: *Baseball:* A game that the starting pitcher finishes.

completion: *Football:* A forward pass that is caught by a receiver. Also called a reception.

compulsory: A routine which all competitors are required to perform. Gymnastics, diving, and figure skating are among the sports that include compulsory (as well as optional) routines.

contact sport: A sport which involves physical contact between opposing players. Football, ice hockey, soccer, boxing, and wrestling are typical contact sports.

Continental grip: *Tennis:* A grip in which the palm of the hand is farther over the handle than in the Eastern forehand grip (in which the palm is behind the handle). The Continental grip is used for hitting slice serves and smashes.

conventional grip: *Bowling:* The normal bowling grip in which the thumb and finger are inserted in the holes up to the second joint. See fingertip grip and semi fingertip grip.

conversion: See point after touchdown.

convert: *Basketball:* To score on a free throw attempt. *Bowling:* To topple all the standing pins with the second ball of a frame, thus scoring a spare. *Football:* To be successful on a try for the point after touchdown. *Soccer:* To score on a penalty kick.

corner area: *Soccer:* The quarter circle with a three-foot radius drawn at each corner of the field. The ball is placed within the corner area for corner kicks.

cornerback: *Football:* Either one of the two defensive backs who plays behind and to the outside of the linebackers, and whose duties include defending against passes and stopping running plays to the outside.

corner kick: *Soccer:* A free kick awarded the attacking team from a corner area when a defender drives the ball beyond his own goal line.

corn snow: *Skiing:* Hard crystals of snow formed by alternating thawing and freezing.

count: *Baseball:* The number of balls and strikes charged to the batter. If there are two balls and two strikes on the batter, the count is 2 and 2. *Bowling:* The number of pins knocked down on the first ball of a frame, and used in figuring the score on a spare in the previous frame.

counter: *Football:* An offensive play in which the ballcarrier slants toward the line in one direction, while the action of the play goes in the direction opposite.

counterpunch: *Boxing:* A punch thrown while blocking an opponent's punch.

court: The open level area, marked with lines, upon which such games as tennis, basketball, handball, and shuffleboard are played.

court tennis: A game which resembles tennis played on a large indoor court surrounded by high cement walls off which the ball may be played.

cover: To defend an area or position.

crackback: *Football:* A block delivered by an offensive player who first heads downfield, then turns back toward the middle of the field to cut down a linebacker or defensive back from the side. The crackback block is illegal.

crampons: *Mountain Climbing:* Steel frames with pointed spikes projecting downward that attach to the bottom of one's boots to prevent slipping when climbing over ice or hard snow.

crawl, crawl stroke: *Swimming:* A stroke executed with the swimmer facedown in the water in which the arms stroke alternately while the legs move rapidly up and down. The swimmer rolls his face to one side to take breaths. In both competitive and recreational swimming, the crawl is the most popular of all strokes.

creel: A wicker basket worn by fishermen for carrying fish.

cricket: An outdoor game played with bats, balls, and wickets by two teams of 11 players each.

croquet: An outdoor game played on a lawn in which players drive wooden balls through a series of wickets using long-handled mallets.

cross: *Boxing:* A hook delivered over an opponent's lead.

crossbar: The horizontal bar that connects the goalposts in football and other goal games. Also, the light bar that rests on pins or small supports and which must be cleared in high jump and vaulting competition.

crossbow: *Archery:* A weapon that consists of a short bow mounted on a wooden frame that resembles a rifle stock. After the bow is drawn, it is released by a trigger.

cross-check: *Ice Hockey:* An illegal check made by holding one's stick in both hands and shoving it across an opponent's body.

cross country: Distance running across open country, rather than following an oval track.

cross-country skiing: The sport of skiing over level terrain, usually through fields and woods. It is more closely related to hiking or backpacking than to downhill skiing. Also called ski touring.

crosse: The stick used in lacrosse.

crossfire: *Baseball:* A sidearm pitch that crosses the plate at an angle.

crossover: *Skating:* A turn that is executed by repeatedly crossing one skate in front of the other.

cross training: Using one sport to practice the techniques of another; for example, using Rollerblading to improve skiing skills.

cue: *Billiards, Pocket Billiards:* The long, thin tapering stick that is used to propel the cue ball.

cue ball: *Billiards, Pocket Billiards:* The white, unnumbered ball that is propelled by the cue.

curl, curl in: *Football:* A pass route in which the receiver runs downfield, then turns back toward the line of scrimmage.

curling: A Scottish game similar to shuffleboard played on ice in which two teams of four players each slide heavy, polished, circular stones toward a fixed mark in the center of a circle at either end of the rink.

curve: *Baseball, Softball:* A pitched ball that breaks to one side and down as it nears the batter. A curve thrown by a right-handed pitcher breaks toward the left. *Bowling:* A bowled ball that breaks from right to left (when delivered by a right-handed bowler) over the full length of the alley.

cushion: *Billiards, Pocket Billiards:* The cloth-covered padding that lines the table's inside rails.

cut: In basketball, football, and other team sports, to make a quick change of direction in an effort to elude an opponent. Also, to drop a prospective player from a roster or team.

cut off: *Baseball:* For an infielder to intercept a ball thrown by an outfielder toward home plate. The infielder then relays the ball to the catcher in an attempt to prevent a run from scoring, or throws to another infielder to prevent the advance of a runner.

cycling: The sport of bicycle racing. See road racing, track racing.

Cy Young Award: An award made annually to the best pitcher in the American League and the National League.

D

daily double: *Horse Racing:* A bet won by choosing both winners of two races, usually the day's first and second races.

darts: A game in which two or more players take turns throwing three darts at a dart board from a distance of nine feet, with points determined by the scoring areas on the board. The object of the game is to score a fixed number of points before one's opponent.

dash: See sprint.

Davis Cup: A trophy awarded to the nation whose team is the winner of the International Lawn Tennis Championship.

day sailer: A small sailboat meant for pleasure sailing and not equipped with sleeping facilities.

dead: Out of play. Said of a ball.

dead heat: A race in which two or more competitors finish at exactly the same time.

dead lift: *Weight Lifting:* A lift in which the weight is lifted from the floor to hip level, often by first straightening the legs, then the back.

dead line: In Canadian football, either of the two lines parallel to and 25 yards behind the goal lines that mark the limits of the playing field.

dead-man's float: *Swimming:* A body position in which the swimmer floats facedown in the water with the arms extended to the side or over the head. Also called prone float.

deadwood: Pins that have been knocked down but remain on the alley or in the gutter. In tenpin bowling, deadwood must be removed before the ball can be rolled. In candlepins, deadwood remains on the alley and is in play.

decathlon: An athletic event in which each contestant participates in 10 different track and field events, including 100-meter and 400-

meter dashes, a distance race, hurdling, shot put, discus, javelin, high jump, long jump, and pole vaulting. Points are awarded on the basis of each athlete's performance in each event, and the winner is the contestant with the highest point total.

decision: *Boxing:* A victory won on points when no knockout has taken place.

decoy: *Hunting:* An artificial bird used to lure live birds to within shooting range.

default: To fail to compete in a contest, which results in a win for the opposition.

defend: To attempt to prevent the opposition from scoring.

defender: *Soccer:* A back whose chief responsibilities are defensive.

defense: Defending against the opposition's attempt to score. Also, the tactical method of defending, that is, the alignment of players, as (in basketball) the 2-1-2 defense, or (in football) the 6-2-3 defense.

defensive back: *Football:* Any one of the four members of the defensive backfield — the two safeties and the two cornerbacks — who are positioned behind the linebackers. It's the job of the defensive backs to defend against passes and give support on running plays.

defensive zone: *Ice Hockey:* The zone in which the goal cage a team is defending is located, and which extends from the goal line to the nearest blue line. One team's defensive zone is the other team's attacking zone. See attacking zone, neutral zone.

deke: *Ice Hockey:* A fake by the puck carrier that enables him to stickhandle around an opponent.

delayed penalty, delayed whistle: *Ice Hockey:* A penalty call that is put off when a foul has been committed by a defending player until the attacking team has shot or lost possession of the puck. To blow the whistle and halt play at the moment the foul is committed would work to penalize the fouled team.

designated hitter: *Baseball:* A player named at the start of the game to bat in place of the pitcher, without causing the pitcher to be removed from the game.

deuce: *Tennis:* A situation in which each player or team has three points (i.e., forty all). A player or team must win two consecutive points to win the game. See advantage.

deuce court: *Tennis:* The service court on the receiver's right. The ball is served into this court whenever the score is deuce.

diamond: *Baseball, Softball:* The infield portion of the playing field. *Billiards, Pocket Billiards:* One of the 18 small diamond-shaped or circular inlays implanted in the rails of the table. They divide each rail into equal parts and are used in figuring the rebound angles of the cue ball or an object ball.

ding: A damaged spot on a surfboard.

dinger: *Baseball:* A home run.

dink: In tennis, volleyball, and other net games, a softly hit ball that goes just beyond the net.

direct free kick: *Soccer:* The free kick awarded a team when an opposing player commits a serious foul, such as kicking, tripping, or holding. The direct free kick is taken from the point of the infraction. A team can score a goal directly with a direct free kick.

discus: *Track and Field:* A disk, usually wood with a metal rim, about eight inches in diameter and weighing approximately four and a half pounds, which is thrown for distance.

discus throw: *Track and Field:* An event in which a discus is hurled for distance with one hand from within a circle approximately eight feet in diameter. Each competitor is permitted three throws in the finals, with the best effort of each determining the final standings.

dismount: *Gymnastics:* Any movement by which the performer gets off a piece of apparatus.

disqualify: To declare a competitor ineligible for competition for breaking certain rules.

distance race: *Track:* Any race of more than a mile.

dive: To plunge headfirst or feet first into the water from a diving board or platform. *Football:* An offensive play in which the ballcarrier plunges headfirst into the line in an attempt for short yardage.

diver's flag: *Scuba Diving:* A red flag with a diagonal white stripe fixed to a boat or float to warn boatmen of the presence of a diver.

diving: A sport in which divers perform a number of optional and compulsory dives, each of which is evaluated and scored by judges. Diving competition is commonly practiced from one- and three-meter diving boards and from the 10-meter platform.

diving board: A flexible board from which a dive is executed, held fast at one end and projecting over the water at the other.

division line: *Basketball:* The line that divides the court in half; also called the midcourt line.

divot: *Golf:* A piece of turf torn up by the club as the ball is struck.

dodo: *Bowling:* A bowling ball that is heavier than the legal weight or one that is not properly balanced.

dogleg: *Golf:* A golf hole in which the fairway is sharply angled to the left or right.

dog paddle: *Swimming:* An elementary swimming stroke in which the swimmer is in a prone position with the head out of the water, the legs and arms submerged. As the legs kick, the hands alternately reach forward and pull back.

dog racing: A sport in which greyhounds pursue a mechanical rabbit about an oval track a quarter to three-eighths of a mile in length. Usually eight dogs compete in a race. The betting system common to horse racing is used.

dolphin kick: *Swimming:* The kick used in performing the butterfly stroke. The legs move up and down together, the knees slightly bent on the upward swing.

double: *Baseball, Softball:* A hit on which the batter reaches second base safely. *Bowling:* Two successive strikes.

double bogey: *Golf:* A stroke score of two strokes over par for a hole.

double-cover: See double-team.

double dribble: *Basketball:* To bounce the ball with both hands at the same time or to stop dribbling and then start again. A double dribble is illegal and results in a loss of possession of the ball.

double eagle: *Golf:* A score of three under par for a hole.

double elimination tournament: A type of tournament common to both individual and team sports in which a player or team is eliminated by losing twice.

double fault: *Tennis:* Two consecutive violations of the service rules resulting in the loss of a point.

double foul: *Basketball:* Two fouls committed at the same time by opposing players against each other. The penalties offset one another, but both players are charged with a foul.

doubleheader: Two games played consecutively on the same program for one admission price.

double pinochle: *Bowling:* A split with the 4, 6, 7, and 10 pins standing.

double play: *Baseball, Softball:* A play in which two players are put out.

doubles: In tennis, platform tennis, badminton, and other court games, a form of play with two players on a side.

doubles court: In tennis, platform tennis, badminton, and other court games, the playing area for doubles. The service courts are the same size as in singles, but once the ball has been put in play by the server, doubles lines for the side boundaries of the court are used giving more room in which to play.

double steal: *Baseball, Softball:* For each of two base runners to steal a base on the same play.

double-team: In football, ice hockey, basketball, and other team sports, to guard or block one opponent with two players. Also called double-cover.

double-up: *Baseball, Softball:* To retire a base runner in the completion of a double play; usually applied to the player retired last.

double wood: *Bowling:* A leave on which one pin remains standing directly behind another.

dowel: *Bowling:* Any of the 10 dark-colored round wooden pins embedded in the lane parallel to the foul line and six to eight feet beyond it. The dowels are used as targets in spot bowling.

down: *Football:* Any of a series of four plays during which time a team must advance at least 10 yards in order to keep possession of the ball.

down-and-in: *Football:* A pass route in which the receiver runs straight downfield, then cuts sharply toward the middle of the field.

down-and-out: *Football:* A pass route in which the receiver runs straight downfield, then cuts sharply toward the sideline.

down box, down indicator: *Football:* A metal rod approximately seven feet long on which is mounted a set of four cards numbered from 1 to 4 which are used to keep track of the number of the down being played. The rod is placed along the sideline to mark where the ball is spotted.

down-the-line shot: *Tennis:* A stroke hit close to and down the length of one of the sidelines.

draft: A selection system common to football, baseball, and other professional sports in which new players are chosen from a pool of available talent, usually ready-to-graduate college players. Teams with poor records are permitted to make their selections before teams with better records.

drag bunt: *Baseball:* A surprise bunt made in an attempt for a base hit. The idea is to "drag" the ball slowly along the ground so the infielders have to rush in and make the play hurriedly.

drag race: A race between cars to determine which can accelerate faster from a standstill.

dragster: A specially built vehicle used in drag racing. It has a light tubular frame with the engine placed in the center of vehicle just ahead of the open cockpit; heavy, wide rear tires; and lightweight, bicycle-type front wheels.

drag strip: A strip of roadway used for drag racing, usually about one-quarter mile long, and wide enough for two vehicles to race side by side.

draw: *Archery:* To pull the string back and tense the bow in preparation for shooting an arrow.

draw: *Billiards, Pocket Billiards:* A shot in which the cue ball is struck below center, which causes it to reverse its path after striking the object ball.

draw: A contest that ends in a tie. Also, the system by which competitors' names are selected at random and matched for tournament play.

draw play: *Football:* An offensive play in which the quarterback drops back as if to pass ("drawing" in the defensive linemen), but then slips the ball to a running back who sifts his way downfield through the onrushing defenders.

draw sheet: The match-by-match listing of tournament competitors prepared as a result of a draw.

draw weight: *Archery:* The force required to pull an arrow to full draw for an arrow of a specific length.

dressage: The guiding of a horse through a series of formal and complex maneuvers by slight movements of the hands, legs, and weight.

dribble: To move a ball by repeated bounces (as in basketball) or light kicks (as in soccer).

drive: *Golf:* A long shot, either from the tee or fairway.

drive in: *Baseball, Softball:* To bat in a run with a hit ball.

driver: *Golf:* A club with a wooden head used in driving from the tee; the number-one wood.

drop: *Baseball:* A pitch that drops suddenly as it nears the plate.

drop kick: *Football:* A kick made by dropping the ball and kicking it just as it rebounds.

drop pass: In basketball or ice hockey, a pass to a trailing teammate. In basketball, the dribbler will suddenly move away from the ball, allowing a teammate to dart forward and take possession. In ice hockey, the puck carrier leaves the puck on the ice for a teammate who is trailing him.

drop shot: In tennis, platform tennis, table tennis, and other net games, a shot hit softly and with backspin that just clears the net and drops suddenly, causing one's opponent to rush forward to make the return.

drop volley: In tennis, platform tennis, table tennis, and other net games, a soft volley that drops just over the net. The drop volley is used chiefly by advanced players.

dub: *Golf:* To hit the ball poorly.

duckpins: A game of bowling common to certain sections of the northeastern United States in which pins that are nine and three-eighths inches in height and balls that are five inches in diameter are used. The alley is the same as in tenpin bowling. A game consists of 10 frames, with three balls to a frame.

duffer: *Golf:* A player who lacks in skill and experience.

dugout: A long, roofed shelter on either side of a baseball field where the players stay when not on the field. A passageway connects the dugout with the team's dressing room.

dump: To lose deliberately.

dunk, dunk shot: *Basketball:* A shot made by leaping high into the air and slamming the ball down through the hoop from above. Also called a stuff shot.

dust-off: *Baseball, Softball:* A pitch that is deliberately thrown high and inside to a batter.

Dutch 200: *Bowling:* A 200 game achieved by bowling strikes and spares alternately.

E

eagle: *Golf:* A score of two below par on a hole.

earned run: *Baseball, Softball:* A run for which the pitcher is responsible. If an error or passed ball contributes to the scoring of a particular run, which would not have scored otherwise, the pitcher is not held responsible for it; the run is unearned.

earned run average: *Baseball, Softball:* A statistic used in rating pitchers, abbreviated ERA, that gives the average number of runs scored against a pitcher per nine-inning game (or, in softball, per seven-inning game). It is determined by dividing the total number of runs allowed by the pitcher by the total number of innings pitched. The result of this division is then multiplied by nine (or, in softball, seven). Thus, a pitcher who is charged with 93 runs for 221 innings has an earned run average of 3.78.

Eastern backhand grip: *Tennis:* A grip in which the palm is placed partly over the handle and the thumb is placed behind the handle.

Eastern forehand grip: *Tennis:* A grip in which the palm of the hand is behind the handle as the ball is stroked.

edge: *Skating:* Either one of the two opposing sides of the skate blade which are in contact with the ice. (The skate blade is made sharp by hollowing a groove along the bottom surface, resulting in the two edges.) Also, the curve that results when a moving edge cuts into the ice. *Skiing:* Either of the two bottom edges of a ski running from tip to tail, often reinforced with metal surfaces. Also, in turning or stopping, to force an edge deeper into the snow by bending the ankle to one side.

eight ball: A pocket billiards game in which one player must pocket the balls numbered one through seven; the other player, those numbered nine through 15. The player who first pockets his object balls and then pockets the eight ball wins the game.

eligible receiver: *Football:* An offensive player who is permitted by the rules to catch a forward pass.

elimination tournament: A tournament in which a single loss can eliminate a player or team from further competition.

encroach: *Football:* To make illegal contact with an opposing player before the snap. Encroaching is illegal and results in a five-yard penalty.

end: *Football:* Either of two players who line up on opposite sides of the offensive or defensive line.

end line: The boundary line at the end of a field or court.

end zone: *Football:* The 10-yard-deep area between the goal line and the end line.

english: *Billiards, Pocket Billiards:* Spin imparted to the cue ball by striking to the right or left of center.

épée: A fencing sword with a long, narrow blade that has no cutting edge and tapers to a blunted point.

error: *Baseball:* A fielding or throwing misplay made when a normal play would have resulted in an out or prevented the advance of a runner. *Bowling:* The failure to convert a spare; a miss, a blow.

exchange: *Track:* In a relay race, to transfer a baton to a teammate.

exchange zone: *Track:* The area 20 meters (65 feet, 7.4 inches) long marked in each lane of a track within which the baton must be exchanged.

exhibition game: An unofficial game played by two professional teams, usually as a part of the preseason training program.

extra-base hit: *Baseball, Softball:* A hit good for more than one base; a double, triple, or home run.

extra point: See point after touchdown.

F

face: *Golf:* The flat part of a club that makes contact with the ball.

face guard, face mask: A protective covering for the face worn by players in a number of sports. In baseball, the face mask is a steel frame held in place by straps and worn by the catcher and umpire. In ice hockey, a molded plastic mask is worn by the goalkeeper. In skin and scuba diving, the face mask is an oval or circular pane of glass or plastic sealed within a flexible rubber frame that fits against the face and is secured by a strap to the back of the head.

face-off: The method of starting play in ice hockey, lacrosse, and other games by releasing the puck or ball between two opposing players.

face-off circle: *Ice Hockey:* One of the five 30-foot circles on the ice within which face-offs are staged.

face-off spot: *Ice Hockey:* One of the four spots, each 12 inches in diameter, within the neutral zone which are used (in addition to the face-off circles) in staging face-offs.

faceplate: The circular or oval pane of glass used in a diver's face mask.

fair catch: *Football:* A catch of a punted ball on the fly by a defensive player who first signals by raising one hand that he will not run with the ball, and who therefore cannot be tackled by members of the kicking team.

fairway: The part of a golf course extending from the tee to the putting green.

falcon: Any of several long-winged hawks or other birds trained to hunt small game.

falconry: The sport of hunting with falcons.

fall: *Wrestling:* The act of throwing or forcing an opponent down on his back.

false start: *Track:* Movement by a competitor off the blocks or across the starting line before the starting signal for a race has been given.

fan: A supporter of a team or an admirer of a particular athlete. *Baseball, Softball:* To strike out.

farm out: To send a player to a farm team.

farm team: A minor league club usually operated by a major league club for the purpose of training young players. Farm teams are common to baseball and ice hockey.

fast: *Horse Racing:* A track that is in first-class condition, permitting horses to run at their fastest.

fastball: *Baseball, Softball:* A pitch thrown at full speed that begins to rise or sink as it nears the plate.

fast break: *Basketball:* An all-out drive toward the opposition goal by members of the offensive team after gaining possession of the ball.

fast pitch softball: A type of softball in which there are no restrictions on the speed of the pitch, except that the ball must be thrown underhand. There are nine players to a team, as in baseball. Base runners are permitted to steal.

fault: In tennis, platform tennis, volleyball, and other court games, a violation of one of the service rules. See double fault.

favorite: A contestant or competitor regarded as the most likely to win.

featherweight: *Boxing:* A fighter weighing between 118 and 127 pounds.

feed: To pass the ball or puck to a teammate who is in a position to score.

feint: Any quick movement by an individual meant to mislead an opponent. One can feint with the head, shoulders, or entire body.

fence posts: *Bowling:* The 7-10 split.

fencing: A sport in which two opponents, each equipped with blunted swords, attack and parry one another's attacks. A bout is conducted on a strip 40 feet long and six feet wide and lasts for six minutes or until one opponent has scored five hits. See foil, épée, saber.

fender: *Boating:* A device — such as an automobile tire, a bundle of rope, or a cylinder-shaped cushion — that is hung over the side of a boat to absorb impact and prevent damage when docking.

field: The playing area for an outdoor game or sport. *Baseball, Softball:* To stop a batted ball and throw it; to retrieve a ball that has been hit into the outfield.

field archery: Competitive archery in which individuals move about a course laid out in a wooded area, shooting a given number of arrows at targets of various sizes at unknown distances.

field arrow: *Archery:* An arrow with a tapered point and large feathers meant for use in field archery.

fielder: *Baseball, Softball:* A player other than the catcher or pitcher who takes up a defensive position in the field while the opposing team is at bat.

fielder's choice: *Baseball, Softball:* A play in which the batter reaches a base safely on an infield ground ball because of the fielder's decision to attempt to put out another runner. The batter is not credited with a hit, but is charged with a time at bat.

field events: The athletic contests conducted within the enclosed field of a running track or near to it, and which include the long jump, high jump, triple jump, pole vault, and such throwing events as the shot put, javelin, and discus.

field goal: *Football:* A score of three points made by place-kicking or drop-kicking the ball over the crossbar between goalposts. *Basketball:* A score of two points made by throwing the ball through the basket.

field hockey: A form of hockey played on a rectangular field between two teams of 11 players. Using curved sticks that vaguely resemble hockey sticks, the players attempt to hit a small ball along the ground and into the opposition goal.

51

fielding average: *Baseball, Softball:* A statistic that indicates a fielder's efficiency and that is determined by first adding the number of putouts, assists, and errors to get total chances; the total chances are then divided into the sum of the putouts and assists. Thus, a player with 440 total chances and 424 putouts and assists has a fielding average of .964.

field judge: A football official who is mainly responsible for covering the play on punts and deep passes.

figure skate: A skate with a shorter than normal blade and tooth-like picks at the front which are used for stopping and spinning.

figure skating: Skating in which competitors trace patterns on the ice and are judged on the form of the patterns as well as their grace and style.

filly: A young female racehorse.

fin: See swim fin.

finals: The last and deciding round of a tournament.

fingertip grip: *Bowling:* A grip in which the fingers are inserted in the ball only up to the first joint, while the thumb is inserted to the normal depth, up to the second joint. See conventional grip, semi fingertip grip.

finish line: An actual or imaginary line across a track that marks the end point of a race.

fireman: *Baseball:* A relief pitcher.

first base: *Baseball, Softball:* The base on the right side of the infield.

first baseman: *Baseball, Softball:* The infielder who is assigned to play to the left of first base and is responsible for covering the base.

first string, first team: The members of a squad who start games and play regularly.

fishhook: A small hook with a barbed point used for catching fish.

fishing: The sport of catching or trying to catch fish. See bait casting, fly casting, spinning, trolling.

fix: To use unlawful tactics in prearranging the outcome of a contest.

flag football: A type of football played with six to nine players to a team in which tackling is not permitted; instead, defensive players must pluck a flag from the ballcarrier's belt to stop him.

flake: A player known for his eccentric conduct.

flanker: *Football:* An offensive player who lines up to the right or left of a formation and usually acts as a pass receiver.

flank vault: *Gymnastics:* A vault in which the gymnast pushes off with one hand and thrusts the legs to one side in going over the horse.

flat: *Football:* The area of the field to the right or left of a formation.

flat out: *Auto Racing:* Traveling at top speed.

flat racing: The sport of racing thoroughbred horses over dirt tracks or oval courses without any barriers to be jumped.

fletching: *Archery:* The feathers fixed to an arrow to stabilize its flight.

flight arrow: *Archery:* An arrow that is thicker in the middle than at the ends and meant for flight shooting.

flight shooting: A type of competitive archery in which individuals seek to shoot their arrows as far as possible.

flipper: See swim fin.

flip shot: *Ice Hockey:* A quick wrist shot in which the puck is lifted into the air.

float: *Fishing:* A small cork or plastic object that is fixed to the line between the bait and the pole and which, by floating, serves to keep the bait at a specific depth. Also called a bobber.

flood: In football, basketball, and other team sports, to send more than one player into the same area of the field or court with the idea of overwhelming the defensive coverage in that area.

floor exercise: *Gymnastics:* A competitive event in which various ballet and tumbling movements are performed on a 40-foot square mat. In women's competition, music accompanies each performance.

flopper: *Ice Hockey:* A goalkeeper who frequently falls to the ice to smother the puck.

flutter kick: *Swimming:* A kick used in the crawl stroke and backstroke in which the legs move up and down alternately without bending at the knees.

fly: *Fishing:* A lure that simulates an insect.

fly ball: *Baseball, Softball:* A ball hit high into the air.

fly casting: A type of fishing in which artificial flies are cast using a lightweight rod and somewhat heavy line.

flying rings: *Gymnastics:* A pair of leather-covered metal rings, seven to 10 inches in diameter, suspended from the ceiling, used in gymnastics competition.

flying start: *Auto Racing:* A start in which the cars, moving in assigned positions, approach the starting line at full speed, or close to it. As the lead car crosses the line, an official waves a green flag, the signal that the race has begun.

fly rod: *Fishing:* A lightweight, flexible fiberglass or split bamboo rod, up to nine and a half feet in length, used in fly casting.

fly tying: The practice of tying various materials to a fishhook to produce artificial flies and other lures. Feathers, fur, and hair are among the materials used.

flyweight: *Boxing:* A boxer of the lightest weight class, weighing 112 pounds or less.

foil: *Fencing:* A sword with a flat guard for the hand and a thin blade with no cutting edge that tapers to a blunted point.

follow: *Billiards, Pocket Billiards:* A shot in which the cue ball is struck above center, which causes it to pursue the object ball after striking it.

football: A game played with a ball on a rectangular field, 100 yards in length, with goal lines and goal posts at either end. Opposing teams of 11 players each attempt to gain possession of the ball and advance it by means of running and passing plays across the opponent's goal line. A team doing so scores a touchdown, worth six points, and then has the opportunity to kick the ball over the goalpost crossbar for one extra point. A field goal — a kick over the crossbar other than when after a touchdown — counts three points. See line of scrimmage, down, forward pass, kick-off, field goal, safety, touchback, touchdown, point after touchdown.

footbed: *Rollerblading:* The padded insole or liner that fits inside the skate boot.

foot fault: In tennis, platform tennis, volleyball, and other court games, a violation of the service rules resulting from illegal placement of the feet.

force-out: *Baseball, Softball:* An out made by tagging a base to which a runner must advance.

forcing shot: *Tennis:* A hard shot that causes one's opponent to hit a weak return.

fore-check: *Ice Hockey:* To check an opponent in his team's defensive zone while he is in control of the puck. Fore-checking is usually done to regain a lost puck or prevent the organization of a play.

forehand: In tennis and other racket sports, a stroke made on the right side of the body by a right-handed player, on the left by a left-handed one.

forfeit: To lose a game or match as a punishment for violating the rules. It can be for such violations as excessive roughness, the refusal to obey an official, or the failure to field a sufficient number of players.

fork ball: *Baseball:* A pitch delivered with the index and middle fingers that drops as it nears the plate.

formation: In football, soccer, and some other team sports, the arrangement of players on either team at the start of play.

formula car: A racing car constructed in accordance with regulations set down by a racing authority.

forward: *Basketball:* Each of two players, members of the front line on offense and defense, and who normally play on either side of the pivotman. *Soccer:* One of five players who make up the forward attacking line. They include the outside right, inside right, center, outside left, and inside left. *Ice Hockey:* Any one of the three players that make up the forward line. They include the right and left wings and the center. *Volleyball:* Any one of the three players stationed close to the net at the time the ball is served.

forward dive: *Diving:* Any dive that begins with the diver facing out from the board or platform.

forward pass: *Football:* A pass thrown in the direction of the opponent's goal.

forward roll: *Gymnastics:* A stunt in which the body rolls in a complete circle, heels over head; a somersault.

foul: *Basketball:* An infraction of the rules for which the penalty is one or more free throws or loss of possession of the ball. Charging and blocking are typical fouls. *Soccer:* A violation of the rules which is penalized by a free kick. Tripping, holding, charging, and using the hands are common fouls. *Bowling:* The act of going beyond the foul line. The penalty is a loss of pinfall on the delivery. *Boxing:* An illegal punch or other illegal action, such as butting or holding. Loss of points can be the result. *Billiards, Pocket Billiards:* A stroke made in violation of the rules for which the penalty is the loss of one's turn. Knocking a ball off the table or shooting the wrong ball are typical fouls.

foul ball: *Baseball, Softball:* A ball hit outside the foul lines.

foul line: *Baseball, Softball:* Either of two straight lines that extend from the rear of home plate to the outer boundary of the outfield, and which indicate the area in which a fair ball may be hit. *Basketball:* The line from which a player takes a foul shot. *Bowling:* The line across the alley 60 feet from the headpin that separates the alley from the approach.

foul out: *Basketball:* To be put out of a game for exceeding the number of fouls permitted. In high school play, a player fouls out after five personal fouls or three technical fouls. *Baseball, Softball:* To be out as a result of a foul ball that is caught.

foul pole: *Baseball, Softball:* Either of two tall poles that mark the foul lines at or near the outer boundaries of a field, and that are used by the umpires to determine whether a batted ball is fair or foul.

foul tip: *Baseball, Softball:* A pitched ball that is deflected back off the bat toward the catcher.

14.1 Continuous: See straight pool.

frame: *Bowling:* A player's turn; also, one of the 10 squares on a score sheet in which the bowler's pinfall is recorded.

free agent: A professional athlete who has the right to deal with any club of his choosing.

free fall: *Skydiving:* The period during a jump before the parachute opens.

free foot; free leg: *Figure Skating:* The foot or leg that is not supporting the body's weight when the skater is on one foot; opposed to skating foot or leg.

free kick: *Soccer:* Any kick awarded to a team after an opposition player has committed a foul or broken a rule. See direct free kick, indirect free kick.

free pass: See intentional walk.

free safety: *Football:* One of the two deepest defensive backs and the one who is free to follow the play wherever it happens to develop. He is not assigned to cover a specific member of the offensive team.

free skating: Competition in which each skater performs a program of his own choosing. Different jumps, spins, and spirals make up the performance.

freestyle: *Swimming:* Competition in which contestants may use a stroke of their own choosing.

free throw: *Basketball:* An unguarded throw to the basket from behind the free-throw line which is awarded a fouled player. A successful free throw counts one point.

free-throw circle: *Basketball:* The circular portion of the free-throw lane, 12 feet in diameter, which encloses the free-throw line.

free-throw lane: *Basketball:* The 12-foot wide area in front of each basket that extends from the baseline to the free-throw line.

free-throw line: *Basketball:* A line 15 feet from the front plane of the backboard. Free throws are attempted from just behind the line. Also called foul line.

freeze: To attempt to retain possession of the ball or puck for an extended period of time without making an effort to score.

frog kick: *Swimming:* A kick used in the breast stroke in which the legs are drawn up close beneath the swimmer's body, then thrust outward together vigorously.

front four: *Football:* The players who make up the four-man defensive front line, that is, the two ends and two tackles.

front grip: See regular grip.

front nine: *Golf:* The first nine holes on an 18-hole course.

fronton: The arena on which jai alai games are held. It includes the court, spectator seating, and betting equipment.

frozen: *Billiards, Pocket Billiards:* The instance of a ball resting against another ball or cushion.

fullback: *Soccer:* One of two primarily defensive players, designated the right and left fullbacks, who normally play nearest the goal the team is defending. *Football:* A member of the offensive backfield. Fullbacks are normally bigger and heavier than halfbacks and are used to block and carry the ball on plunges into the line.

full gainer: *Diving:* A forward dive in which the diver executes a full backward somersault.

full nelson: *Wrestling:* A hold in which both arms are passed under the opponent's arms from behind, then pressed against the back of the neck.

fumble: *Football:* To drop a ball that is in play.

fungo: *Baseball:* A practice fly hit to a fielder by tossing the ball in the air and hitting it as it falls.

fungo bat: *Baseball:* A thinner than normal bat with a short barrel and long handle designed for hitting fungoes.

furlong: *Horse Racing:* A distance equal to one-eighth of a mile.

G

gainer: *Diving:* A dive in which the diver leaves the board facing forward, performs a back somersault, and enters the water feet first.

gait: Any of the ways a horse may travel by lifting the feet in a different sequence or rhythm.

gallop: A horse's natural three-beat gait, which is faster than a canter and slower than a run.

game: *Tennis:* A unit of competition scored in points. Four points are needed to win one game.

game ball: *Football:* A ball that members of a winning team award to a player or coach in recognition of his contribution to the team's success.

gamecock: A rooster trained for cockfighting.

game misconduct penalty: *Ice Hockey:* A penalty in which the guilty player is suspended for the remainder of the game.

gate: A pair of markers between which competitors must pass in a slalom race. In skiing, the gates take the form of vertical poles. In water skiing, the gates are anchored buoys.

giant slalom: *Skiing:* A ski race over a long downhill course with a vertical drop of at least 1,000 feet, and one that offers less than half of the gates to be found in a standard slalom course.

glider: An aircraft without an engine that rides rising currents of air.

glove: The oversized padded leather covering for the hand, usually with a separate section for each finger, used in catching a ball or stopping a puck.

goal: The structure or area over which or into which the ball or puck must be driven for a score.

goal area: *Soccer:* The rectangular area just in front of each goal that is 20 yards wide and six yards deep.

goal crease: *Ice Hockey:* The rectangular area just in front of each goal that is eight feet wide and four feet deep. Members of the attacking team are not permitted within the goal crease unless the puck is in it.

goal judge: *Ice Hockey:* Either of two officials posted behind the goals who signal when the puck crosses the goal line. It is the referee, however, who makes the final decision on whether a goal has been scored.

goalkeeper, goaltender, goalie: The player assigned to protect the goal.

goal kick: *Soccer:* The kick used to put the ball back in play when a member of the attacking team has caused the ball to go over the goal line (but not into the goal). The ball is placed down in that half of the goal nearest to where the ball crossed the goal line. A member of the defending team then kicks the ball upfield through the penalty area.

goal light: *Ice Hockey:* The red light mounted behind each goal that is lighted by the goal judge when a goal is scored.

goal line: *Football:* The line at each end of and running the width of the playing field 10 yards from the end line and over which the ball must be carried or passed to score a touchdown. *Soccer:* The line at each end of and running the width of the playing field in the center of which the goal is located. *Ice Hockey:* The line that extends across each end of the rink 10 to 15 feet from the end boards, in the center of which the goal is located.

goal-line stand: *Football:* A strong defensive effort in which the opposition's repeated attempts to score from very close to the goal line are turned back.

goalmouth: *Ice Hockey:* The open area of a goal between the goalposts.

goalpost: Either of two posts joined by a crossbar that forms the goal in soccer, ice hockey, and many other team sports.

goaltending: *Basketball:* Interfering with a shot by a defensive player who touches the ball which is on its downward flight to the basket, or who touches the rim of the basket or the ball while the ball is within the rim. Goaltending is illegal.

gold medal: In the Olympic Games and other sports competition, the gold or gold-colored medal awarded the winner of an event.

golf: A game played on a large outdoor course in which each participant, using a variety of clubs, attempts to drive a small ball into a succession of holes, using as few strokes as possible.

golf club: A club with a long slender shaft and small wooden or steel head with which the ball is struck. There are 14 clubs in a full set — four woods, nine irons, and a putter.

golf widow: A woman whose husband spends a great amount of time on the golf course.

gondola: *Skiing:* An enclosed car that is suspended from a moving overhead cable and used to transport skiers to the top of a slope.

gopher ball: *Baseball, Softball:* A pitch that is hit for a home run.

Grand Prix: Any of several international road races for sports cars of a specific engine size. The term Grand Prix is French for grand prize.

grand slam: *Baseball, Softball:* A home run with the bases filled.

grandstand: A roofed stand for spectators at a stadium or race track.

grandstand play: A play that is performed to impress spectators.

grapefruit league: *Baseball:* The exhibition game competition in spring training among teams that train in Florida.

grass cutter: *Baseball, Softball:* A hard-hit ball that skims along the ground.

green: See putting green.

green flag: *Auto Racing:* A flag used to signal drivers that a race has officially started. A green flag is also used following a yellow caution flag to tell the drivers that they can resume normal speed.

greens fee: *Golf:* The payment made for the right to play a golf course.

Grey Cup: The trophy awarded to the championship team in the Canadian Football League.

greyhound: A large, slender dog, with a smooth coat, narrow back, and long legs used for racing.

grid: *Auto Racing:* The starting position of cars on a track.

gridiron: A football field.

groom: *Horse Racing:* A stable hand who is charged with the care of a horse. *Skiing:* To prepare a slope by smoothing or packing down the snow.

grounding: *Golf:* Touching the head of the club to the ground while preparing to swing. Grounding is not permitted when the ball is being played from a sand trap or other hazard. The penalty is two strokes. *Football:* See intentional grounding.

ground out: *Baseball, Softball:* To be thrown out at first base after hitting a ground ball to an infielder.

ground rule: *Baseball, Softball:* A rule adopted to fit a particular situation. A ground rule, for example, may state how many bases a runner can advance when a batted ball bounces into the stands.

ground stroke: *Tennis:* Any stroke used in hitting the ball after a full bounce.

guard: *Basketball:* Either of two players who are often positioned farthest from the basket and are responsible for bringing the ball downcourt on planned offensive plays. *Football:*

Either of two offensive players who are positioned on either side of the center. Guards create holes for the ballcarrier on plunges into the line, pull from the line to lead the ballcarrier on sweeps, and protect the quarterback on pass plays.

gun dog: *Hunting:* A dog trained to assist hunters, as in flushing or retrieving game. Pointers and setters are popular gun dogs.

gun lap: *Track:* The final lap of a race signaled by the firing of a gun.

gunner: *Basketball:* A player who shoots continually, even when a teammate may be in a more favorable scoring position.

gutter: *Bowling:* The trough on either side of the alley that catches balls that leave the alley and leads them into the pit.

gutter ball: *Bowling:* A ball that rolls off the alley and into the gutter, or trough. A gutter ball is a dead ball and counts as a turn.

gymkhana: *Riding:* A riding competition featuring games and contests rather than the usual horse show events.

gymnastics: A sport in which individuals perform a variety of acrobatic feats that stress grace, precision, flexibility, balance, and body control. In competitive gymnastics, there are different events for men and women. The men's events include the parallel bars, pommel horse, horizontal bar, flying rings, and floor exercise. Women's events are the balance beam, vaulting horse, uneven bars, and floor exercise.

H

hack: *Basketball:* To strike an opponent's arm.

hacker: *Tennis:* A player lacking in skill and experience.

halfback: *Football:* A player who, along with the fullback, lines up behind the quarterback. He frequently carries the ball or blocks and occasionally catches passes. *Soccer:* Any of three players whose chief responsibilities are defensive, but also take part in the attack, often by triggering an offensive thrust. Halfbacks are designated right, center, and left.

half nelson: *Wrestling:* A hold in which the arm is passed under the opponent's arm from behind to the back of his neck.

halftime: The intermission between halves of a game such as in basketball or football.

half volley: In tennis, platform tennis, handball, and other court games, a stroke made just as the ball rebounds from the playing surface.

halfway line: *Soccer:* The line across the field that divides the field into two equal parts.

halve: *Golf:* To play a hole in the same number of strokes as one's opponent.

hammer: *Track and Field:* The metal ball, weighing approximately 16 pounds and connected by a four-foot steel wire to a loop grip, that is thrown in the hammer throw.

hammerlock: *Wrestling:* A hold in which the opponent's arm is pulled behind his back and twisted upward.

hammer throw: *Track and Field:* A field event in which the hammer is thrown for distance. Each contestant throws from within a seven-foot circle, grasping the grip in both hands, spinning three or four times, then letting the hammer fly.

handball: A wall game played by two players or two teams of two players each in which a small rubber ball weighing two ounces is batted against the wall with the hand, usually with a special glove. There are one-wall, three-wall, and four-wall varieties of handball. In each, the idea is to make a shot the opposition cannot return to the front wall. The first player or team to score 21 points wins the game.

handicap: An advantage given to a weaker opponent to equalize competition. In golf, a handicap can be a number of strokes given an opponent. In bowling, the handicap can be pins added to the opponent's score. In a horse race, handicapping involves adjusting the number of pounds each horse must carry.

hand off: *Football:* To hand the ball to a teammate. Most plays begin with the quarterback handing off to a running back.

hand ride: *Horse Racing:* To ride a horse in a race without using either a whip or spurs.

handspring: *Gymnastics:* A stunt in which the body is flipped forward or backward from an upright position, with the performer landing first on the hands, then on the feet.

handstand: *Gymnastics:* Balancing on one's hands with the feet directly over the head.

hang: *Baseball, Softball:* Said of a pitch that fails to break.

hang five: *Surfing:* To ride the board with the body's weight forward and the toes of one foot curled over the end of the board.

hang glider: A small, light, engineless craft from which a rider hangs for soaring.

hang 10: *Surfing:* To ride the board with the body forward and the toes of both feet over the end of the board.

hang time: *Football:* The amount of time a punted ball remains in the air.

harness racing: The sport of racing horses harnessed to lightweight two-wheeled vehicles called sulkies. A special breed of horses, known as standardbreds, have been developed for the sport.

harrier: A runner on a cross-country team.

hashmark: See inbound line.

hat trick: Three goals by one player in one game. The term is common to ice hockey and soccer.

hazard: *Golf:* A sand trap or other obstacle.

head: *Soccer:* To drive the ball by striking it with one's head. *Billiards, Pocket Billiards:* The end of the table that bears the manufacturer's nameplate, and from where a player shoots the break shot. *Golf:* The hitting end of the club. *Tennis:* The oval part of the racket that holds the strings. *Horse Racing:* The length of a horse's head used to express the margin of victory in a close race.

header: A headfirst dive.

head linesman: *Football:* The official who is responsible for watching for offside violations and illegal formations, and who marks where the ball goes out of bounds.

headlock: *Wrestling:* A hold in which the head of one wrestler is locked under the arm of the other.

head-man: *Ice Hockey:* To pass the puck ahead of an attacking teammate, usually a center or wing.

headpin: *Bowling:* The number 1 pin.

headstall: *Horseback Riding:* The section of the bridle that fits over the horse's head.

headstand: *Gymnastics:* A stunt in which one balances on the head and hands, the feet directly overhead.

heat: A preliminary race to determine finalists. Heats are common to track and swimming.

heavy: *Horse Racing:* A track that is very muddy.

heavy bag: *Boxing:* A large stuffed canvas or leather bag suspended from the ceiling and used by a boxer in developing punching power.

heavy hit: *Bowling:* A bowled ball that goes just beyond the 1-3 pocket, hitting more squarely on the 3 pin than on the 1 pin.

heavyweight: *Boxing:* The heaviest weight boxing class; also a boxer weighing more than 175 pounds.

heel kick: *Soccer:* A kick made by driving the ball backward with the heel.

held ball: *Basketball:* A situation in which two opposing players struggle for the ball without either being able to gain full possession. Play is halted and a jump ball is called. Also called tie ball.

helm: The wheel or tiller of a boat; the steering gear.

helmet: The head covering of hard material, such as leather or plastic, worn while participating in many sports — football, ice hockey, baseball (when batting), lacrosse, and boxing.

herringbone: *Skiing:* A method of climbing a slope with the tips of the skis pointed outward, thus making a fishbone pattern in the snow.

high board: *Diving:* A diving board placed three meters (9.8 feet) above the water.

high hurdles: A race run over hurdles that are 39 inches in height in high school competition, 42 inches otherwise. Common indoor distances are 50 yards (four hurdles) and 60 yards (five hurdles). Outdoor distances are 120 yards (10 hurdles) and 110 meters (10 hurdles).

high jump: *Track and Field:* An event in which competitors jump for height over an adjustable crossbar.

high sticking: *Ice Hockey:* Carrying the blade of one's stick above shoulder level or striking an opponent with the blade while held at such a level. A major penalty can be the result.

hip check: *Ice Hockey:* A body check in which a player drives into an opponent with his hip.

hip circle: *Gymnastics:* A stunt in which the performer swings around a horizontal bar, the arms straight, the belly and hips held against the bar.

hit: *Baseball, Softball:* To bat; a base hit.

hit-and-run: *Baseball:* A play in which the runner on first base breaks for second base as the pitch is delivered, and the batter tries to hit the pitch. Often the batter will poke the ball into the area vacated by either the second baseman or shortstop, who is darting over to cover second base in an effort to prevent a steal.

hitch-and-go: *Football:* A pass route in which the runner breaks straight downfield, fakes to the right or left as if he is about to catch a short pass, then races farther downfield.

hockey: See field hockey, ice hockey.

hockey skate: A skate with a blade of medium length (longer than a figure skate blade and shorter than a speed skate blade). The boot features a hard box toe, and the heel extends high in the back to protect the muscles of the lower calf.

hold, holding: In football and some other team sports, using one's hands to restrict the movement of an opposing player.

holder: *Football:* The player assigned to hold the ball upright for the kicker on field-goal and extra-point attempts.

hole: *Football:* The opening between two linemen through which the ballcarrier plunges.

Golf: The circular depression, four and a half inches in diameter, into which the ball is putted.

hole-in-one: *Golf:* Driving the ball from the tee into the hole in only one stroke.

home plate: *Baseball, Softball:* The five-sided slab of white rubber that serves as a final base to be touched by a runner in scoring a run.

homer, home run: *Baseball, Softball:* A hit that enables the batter to make a complete circuit of the bases and score a run.

home stand: In various professional sports, a number of consecutive games played in a team's home park or arena.

homestretch: That portion of a race track from the last turn to the finish line.

honor: *Golf:* The right of being the first to drive the ball from the tee. The honor goes to the player having the fewest strokes on the previous hole.

hook: *Baseball, Softball:* A curve ball. *Bowling:* A ball that travels straight down the alley, then abruptly veers toward the pins as it nears them. See curve ball, back-up ball. *Boxing:* A short, bent-arm blow that travels in an arc. *Golf:* A shot in which the ball travels off course to the left (for a right-handed golfer). See slice.

hook check: *Ice Hockey:* A stick check usually executed from behind the puck carrier in which one's stick is put almost flat to the ice, then swept toward an opposing player in an attempt to snare the puck from his stick.

hook shot: *Basketball:* A shot made with the body sideways to the basket, the outstretched right arm sweeping upward with the ball, the right hand releasing it at the highest point of its arc.

hook slide: *Baseball, Softball:* A slide made by leaning away from the base and hooking it with the instep of an extended foot.

hoop: *Basketball:* The metal rim of the basket, 18 inches in diameter.

hop, step, and jump: See triple jump.

horizontal bar: *Gymnastics:* A metal bar approximately eight feet long and eight feet off the floor used in the performance of a variety of acrobatic skills in men's gymnastics competition.

horse: *Gymnastics:* See pommel horse, vaulting horse.

horsehide: A baseball.

horse racing: The sport of racing specially bred horses called thoroughbreds over distances of from a half to one and a half miles.

horseshoe: A U-shaped piece of metal approximately seven and a half inches in length, and weighing up to two and a half pounds, that is pitched in the game of horseshoes.

horseshoes: A game in which two opposing players or two teams of two players each take turns in attempting to toss two horseshoes around a metal stake 40 feet away. To do so is to score a ringer, which counts three points. A side also receives one point for each shoe it gets closer to the stake than the opposition. Games are usually played to 50 points in singles, to 21 points in doubles.

hot corner: *Baseball, Softball:* Third base.

hotdog: A player who performs in a flashy manner.

house ball: *Bowling:* A ball that is provided by the bowling center.

huddle: *Football:* A brief gathering among members of the offensive or defensive teams in order to receive instructions for the upcoming play.

hunting bow: *Archery:* A bow with a higher than normal draw weight that is used in hunting game.

hurdle: *Track:* A light, portable, wooden or metal barrier which consists of two vertical posts between which a horizontal bar is fixed. *Gymnastics:* In vaulting and some tumbling exercises, the short spring made on the last step of the approach that takes the gymnast to the take-off point.

hurdles, hurdle race: *Track:* A race in which a series of hurdles must be jumped. See low hurdles, high hurdles, intermediate hurdles.

hurley: The stick used in the game of hurling.

hurling: An Irish game that resembles field hockey or lacrosse that is played on a large rectangular field between two teams of 15 players, each player using a broad-bladed stick to catch and hold the ball while running. The object of the game is to drive the ball into the opponent's goal for a score.

hustler: An individual who seeks to induce persons less skilled than himself to gamble at pool or billiards.

hydroplane: A powerboat designed so that the hull lifts out of the water and skims the surface at high speeds.

I

ice, icing: *Ice Hockey:* Intentionally shooting the puck across the rink's center line and over the opponent's goal line. Icing is an infraction; play must be restarted with a face-off.

iceboat: A boat-like vehicle set on runners that sails on the ice.

ice dancing: *Figure Skating:* Competition in which each couple performs such ballroom dances as the fox trot, waltz, and tango to music on ice.

ice fishing: The sport of fishing through a hole chopped in the ice of a frozen lake.

ice hockey: A game played on the ice in which two opposing teams of six players wearing ice skates and using thin-bladed sticks attempt to drive a hard rubber puck into the opposition goal. A game consists of three 20-minute periods. See icing, offside, major penalty, minor penalty, face-off.

ice time: *Ice Hockey:* The amount of playing time accumulated by a player during a game or season.

illegal motion: *Football:* Movement by a member of the offensive team (other than the man in motion) after the team is set and before the ball is snapped. Illegal motion is an infraction that results in a five-yard penalty.

illegal procedure: *Football:* An instance in which the offensive team is guilty of one of several rule violations, including an illegal shift, illegal formation, or the failure to pause one second after the huddle. The result is a five-yard penalty.

inboard boat: A boat in which the engine is inside the hull.

in bounds: Within the playing field.

inbound line: *Football:* One of the two short lines that intersect each of the field's yard lines to indicate where the ball is to be placed following a play that has gone wide to the left or right. Also called a hashmark.

incompletion: *Football:* A forward pass not caught in bounds or intercepted.

Indianapolis 500: A 500-mile race for single-seat, rear-engine racing cars run annually since 1911 at the Indianapolis Motor Speedway.

Indian club: A bottle-shaped wooden club swung in the hand for exercise.

Indian wrestling: A type of leg wrestling in which opponents lie on their backs side by side, their feet facing in opposite directions, and attempt to roll each other backwards by hooking their near legs and applying pressure.

indirect free kick: *Soccer:* The free kick awarded a team for what is considered a minor offense by the opposition. It can be for arguing with the referee, coaching from the sidelines, or for an offside violation. The kick is taken from the point of the infraction. A team cannot score a goal directly from the kick; the ball must be played by at least one player.

individual medley: *Swimming:* A race in which each competitor must swim each leg of the race with a different stroke. The strokes used are the butterfly, backstroke, breast stroke, and freestyle. Usual distances for the individual medley are 200 and 400 yards, and 200 and 400 meters.

Indy car: A single-seat, rear-engine racing car, built low to the ground, that competes at the Indianapolis 500 and more than a dozen other races each year. The world's fastest racers, Indy cars are capable of speeds over 230 miles per hour.

infield: *Baseball, Softball:* The area of the field enclosed by the foul line and the arc of the outfield grass just beyond the bases. *Track, Horse Racing, Auto Racing:* The area enclosed by the race course.

infielder: *Baseball, Softball:* A player who plays in the infield; the first, second, or third baseman, or the shortstop.

infield fly: *Baseball, Softball:* A fair fly ball hit within the infield area when less than two are out and runners are on first and second bases, or first, second, and third. If, in the judgment of the umpire, the ball can be caught with normal effort, the batter is automatically out. This prevents a situation in which an infielder deliberately does not catch the ball in order to attempt a double play.

infield hit: *Baseball, Softball:* A base hit in which the ball does not leave the infield.

infraction: Any breach of the playing rules.

in-line skating: Another term for Rollerblading. It also refers to the arrangement of the wheels — in a single straight line — beneath the boot.

inning: *Baseball:* One of nine divisions of a regular game in which each team has a turn at bat that ends when three players have been put out. *Billiards, Pocket Billiards:* A player's turn. *Bowling:* A frame.

inside: *Football:* Toward the center of the field.

inside edge: *Figure Skating:* The edge of the skate blade nearest the other skate.

inside left: *Soccer:* The forward who is positioned between the center forward and the right wing.

intentional foul: *Basketball:* A personal foul committed deliberately by a member of the defensive team. An intentional foul is resorted to by a team that is trailing in the late stages of a game. The calling of the foul stops the clock and the ensuing free throw gives the defensive team the chance to regain possession.

intentional grounding: *Football:* A deliberate attempt by a quarterback to throw the ball out of bounds or so that it hits the ground; the result is an incomplete forward pass. A quarterback grounds the ball to avoid being thrown for a loss. Intentional grounding can result in the loss of the down and a 15-yard penalty.

intentional walk: *Baseball, Softball:* A base on balls deliberately given to an opposing batter. The pitcher may want to avoid pitching to a good hitter or be attempting to set up a force play at second base.

interception: *Football:* A forward pass that is caught by the opposition.

interlocking grip: *Golf:* A method of gripping the golf club in which the forefinger of the left hand interlocks with the little finger of the right hand. See Vardon grip, baseball grip.

intermediate hurdles: *Track:* A race over hurdles that are 36 inches in height. Distances for such races are usually 330 yards (eight hurdles), 400 meters (10 hurdles), or 440 yards (10 hurdles).

interval training: *Track and Field:* A method of conditioning that involves alternately running and jogging over set distances.

invitational: A contest or meet open only to invited participants.

inward dive: *Diving:* Any of a group of dives which are begun with the diver facing the diving board.

iron: *Golf:* A club with a metal head, normally used for fairway and approach shots. Irons are numbered from one to nine. The higher the number, the greater the degree of slant of the face of the club. The greater the slant, the higher and shorter the flight of the ball.

isometric exercise: A form of conditioning in which one's muscles are made to strain against some immovable object, such as a wall or door frame.

isotonic exercise: A form of conditioning in which one's muscles are made to strain against some movable object, such as a barbell.

J

jab: *Boxing:* A quick, straight blow, usually delivered to the opponent's head with the lead hand (the left hand in the case of a right-handed boxer).

J bar: *Skiing:* A ski lift in which a J-shaped bar suspended from an overhead cable is used to pull the skier to the top of the slope.

jack: *Lawn Bowling:* The small white ball, two and a half inches in diameter, that serves as the bowler's target.

jackknife: *Diving:* A dive executed by jumping headfirst and then bending at the waist to form a 90-degree angle; the legs are kept straight. The diver then reaches forward to touch the feet with the hands before straightening out to enter the water, hands first.

Jacob's ladder: *Boating:* A rope or chain ladder with rigid steps.

jam: *Baseball, Softball:* To pitch inside to a batter, usually very close to his hands, to prevent him from hitting the ball solidly.

jammer: *Roller Derby:* A competitor who breaks away from the pack and attempts to lap members of the opposing team to score points.

javelin: *Track and Field:* A metal-tipped wooden or metal spear, eight and a half to nine feet in length, used in the javelin throw.

javelin throw: *Track and Field:* A field event in which the javelin is thrown for distance.

jerk: *Weight Lifting:* The second phase of the clean and jerk in which the weight is lifted from shoulder height to an over-the-head position with the arms upraised. See clean and jerk.

Jersey: See Brooklyn.

jib: *Sailing:* A triangular sail set forward of the mast.

jock: An athlete interested only in sports.

jockey: *Horse Racing:* A person who rides a thoroughbred in a race. Light weight is essential to be a jockey, and most weigh between 100 and 115 pounds.

jog: To run at a steady slow trot.

judo: An Oriental form of wrestling developed from jujitsu which employs principles of balance and leverage. See jujitsu.

jujitsu: An Oriental art of self-defense or hand-to-hand combat which employs throwing techniques and blows to vulnerable parts of the body.

juke: *Football:* To fake an opponent, especially a potential tackler, out of position.

jump ball: *Basketball:* The method of putting the ball in play in which the referee tosses the ball up between two opposing players who leap and attempt to tap the ball to a teammate. A jump ball is used at the beginning of a period, when a held ball is called, or when the referee is unable to determine which side last touched the ball before it went out of bounds.

jumped ball: *Billiards, Pocket Billiards:* A ball that is knocked from the table.

jumper: *Track and Field:* A competitor in a jumping event, such as the high jump or long jump. *Basketball:* A jump shot.

jump shot: *Basketball:* A shot in which the ball is released at the top of a jump. *Billiards, Pocket Billiards:* A legal shot in which the ball is sent up into the air to clear a ball that blocks its path.

jump the gun: To start a race before the starting signal.

junk: *Baseball:* Pitches that are regarded as being of inferior quality, usually slow curveballs.

juvenile: A two-year-old racehorse.

J valve: *Scuba Diving:* A valve that regulates the flow of air from the diver's air tanks and features an automatic shutoff to warn him that his air supply is running low. The diver then pulls a lever to release the air that remains in the tank. See K valve.

K

K: *Baseball, Softball:* A strikeout. The symbol K is used in scoring a game to indicate a strikeout.

karate: An Oriental system of self-defense that stresses crisply delivered kicks and punches.

kart: A midget automobile used in racing.

karting: The sport of racing karts. There are several classes of competition based on drivers' ages and engine types and sizes.

kayak: A lightweight, highly maneuverable canvas-covered canoe, pointed at both ends, and covered except for an open area where the paddler sits.

keel: The main structural beam of a boat that runs fore and aft on the center line.

kegler: A bowler.

Kentucky Derby: An annual mile and a quarter race for three-year-old thoroughbreds run since 1875 at Churchill Downs in Louisville, Kentucky.

key: *Football:* To observe an opposing player closely to determine the direction in which he will be moving. A running back, for example, who draws his left foot back slightly as he lines up, may be going to carry the ball to the right. Keying on the back can reveal this.

key, keyhole: *Basketball:* The entire free-throw area. It includes the free-throw lane and the

free-throw circle. See free-throw lane, free-throw circle.

kick: *Football:* To score or attempt to score a field goal or point after touchdown by kicking the ball. *Track:* To put on a burst of speed during a race, usually toward the finish.

kickback: *Bowling:* Each of the two vertical partitions that frame the sides of the alley at the pindeck and extend into the pit. Pins often rebound from the kickback to knock down other pins.

kickball: A variation of baseball common to playgrounds and schoolyards. Instead of a baseball being hit with a bat, an inflated rubber ball is kicked.

kickboard: *Swimming:* A board about 30 inches in length, frequently made of styrofoam, that is grasped by a beginner with both hands to support the upper body as leg kicks are being practiced. Also called a paddleboard.

kicking game: *Football:* That part of a team's offensive planning that involves punting and place-kicking.

kicking tee: See tee.

kickoff: *Football:* To put the ball in play by place-kicking it toward the opposing team. *Soccer:* To start play by having one player kick the ball to a teammate. Members of the opposing team can be no closer than 10 yards to the player kicking off.

kickoff circle: *Soccer:* The circle that is 20 yards in diameter at the center of the field from within which kickoffs are made.

kick save: *Ice Hockey:* A save by the goalkeeper in which the puck is deflected with the skate or the pads of the lower leg.

kick serve: *Tennis:* A serve that causes the ball to swerve abruptly to the right or left after bouncing.

kick turn: *Skiing:* A method of turning 180 degrees from a standing position. One ski is kicked up until only the tail of the ski touches the ground; the leg is then swung out and around and the ankle rotated so that the ski can be placed on the snow near its original position, but facing in the opposite direction. The other ski is then lifted and brought parallel to the first.

kill shot: In tennis and other racket games, a shot hit with such force that it is virtually unreturnable. Sometimes called a smash.

kingpin: *Bowling:* The number 5 pin. The ball must hit the 5 pin in order for a strike to be achieved.

kip: *Gymnastics:* In swinging from a horizontal bar, a movement at the end of the swing in which the performer snaps the legs back and straightens them, then raises the body to an arm support position.

kiss: *Billiards, Pocket Billiards:* A shot in which the cue ball rebounds from one object ball to another.

knockdown: *Boxing:* To send an opponent to the canvas, but not necessarily knocking him out.

knock out: *Boxing:* To render an opponent unconscious. Also, to defeat an opponent by knocking him to the canvas for a count of 10. *Baseball:* To cause an opposing pitcher to be removed from the game by heavy hitting.

knot: A measure of speed used on boats that is equal to one nautical mile (6,080 feet) per hour.

knuckleball, knuckler: *Baseball:* A slow, fluttering pitch that is thrown by gripping the ball with the knuckles of two or three fingers.

knuckle curve: *Baseball:* A curveball that is thrown with a knuckleball grip.

kung fu: A Chinese art of self-defense that is similar to karate.

K valve: *Scuba Diving:* A valve that regulates the flow of air from the diver's tanks, but has no device to warn that the air supply is running out. See J valve.

L

lacrosse: A game resembling field hockey that is played on a rectangular field between two teams of 10 players using long-handled sticks with triangular pockets at one end. The object of the game is to move the ball toward the opponent's goal by running with it or passing it, then throwing it or kicking it past the goalkeeper.

ladder tournament: A type of tournament common to tennis in which participants are first ranked according to estimated strengths, the best player at the top. Any player can then challenge the players ranked ahead of him. When a challenger wins, he exchanges "rungs" on the ladder with the defeated player. At the tournament's end, rankings reflect the actual strength of participants.

lag, lagging: *Billiards, Pocket Billiards:* The method of determining the order of play. Each participant in turn shoots the cue ball from the head of the table to the rail at the opposite end, and the player who rebounds the ball closest to the rail at the head of the table has a choice of breaking or assigning his opponent to break.

lane: *Swimming:* The parallel courses at least six feet in width, marked by ropes strung between buoys, within which contestants must stay during a race. *Track:* The parallel courses, usually four feet in width, marked on a track within which competitors must stay during a sprint. *Basketball:* See free-throw lane. *Bowling:* The bowling alley. See alley.

lap: One complete circuit of a race course or the length of a swimming pool from one end to the other. Also, to overtake and come to lead an opponent by a length of the race course.

lateral, lateral pass: *Football:* A pass thrown to the side or backward, that is, other than in the direction in which the team is attempting to advance.

lawn bowling: A game in which one rolls hard rubber or composition balls over a smooth, grassy surface toward a small, white ball that is known as a jack. Points are scored by the individual or team placing its balls closest to the jack.

layout: A body position common to gymnastics and diving in which the body is fully extended, the legs together and straight, the back arched, the arms held up and back.

lay-up: *Basketball:* A shot made close to the basket in which the ball is played off the backboard.

lead: The margin by which a team or an individual is ahead. *Baseball:* The distance a base runner advances off base toward the next base. The runner stays just close enough to the base to be able to get back quickly should the opposing pitcher or catcher make an attempt to pick him off.

lead off: *Baseball, Softball:* To bat first for a team in the batting order or in an inning.

league: An association of teams that compete among themselves in a season of regularly scheduled games.

leave: *Bowling:* The pins left standing after the first ball has been rolled in a frame.

leeward: *Boating:* The side away from the wind.

left field: *Baseball, Softball:* The left side of the outfield as viewed from home plate; the outfield area beyond third base.

left fielder: *Baseball, Softball:* The player who plays left field.

leg: *Track, Swimming:* The portion of a relay race that each member of the relay team must cover. *Sailing:* The distance traveled by a boat on a single tack.

length: A unit of measurement based on the approximate front to back distance of an animal or vehicle in a race.

let: A stroke in tennis, volleyball, badminton, and other net games that does not count and must be repeated. For example, a let is called in tennis when a serve strikes the net before landing in the service court.

letter: An initial or a design based on one or more letters that represents the name of a school or college, and which is awarded to a student for participating in a particular sport.

letterman: A player on a school or college team who has been awarded a letter in a sport.

letup: See change-up.

lie: *Golf:* The position of a ball after it comes to a stop. *Ice Hockey:* The angle between the blade of the stick and the handle or shaft as expressed on a numerical scale. A lie four stick has a wide blade-to-handle angle. A lie eight stick has a smaller angle. Lies four and five are average lies.

light hit: *Bowling:* A bowled ball that just fails to hit the 1-3 pocket solidly, hitting more squarely on the 1 pin than the 3 pin.

lightweight: *Boxing:* A fighter weighing between 127 and 135 pounds.

limit: The maximum number of fish, birds, or other game permitted by law to be taken during a specified period.

line: A narrow white marking, often one and a half to two inches in width, on a court or field that indicates the boundary of play. *Bowling:*

A game; 10 frames. *Fishing:* The string or cord used in catching fish. The bait, fly, or lure is cast into the water and drawn back by means of the line. *Baseball, Softball:* To hit the ball sharply; to hit a line drive. *Football:* See line of scrimmage. *Basketball:* See free-throw line.

linebacker: *Football:* Any of the usually three defensive players forming a second line of defense behind the ends and tackles.

line drive, liner: *Baseball, Softball:* A ball hit sharply so that its path is approximately a straight line.

line judge: *Football:* An official posted near one of the sidelines to assist the referee, and who is chiefly responsible for watching for offside violations and the position of the quarterback on pass plays. (The quarterback is not permitted to cross the line of scrimmage on passes.) The line judge is also the game's timekeeper.

lineman: *Football:* Any of the offensive or defensive players positioned on the forward line.

line of scrimmage: *Football:* An imaginary line across the field through the forward point of the ball at which the opposing teams line up for a new play.

line out: *Baseball, Softball:* To hit a line drive that is caught for an out.

line score: *Baseball, Softball:* A brief summary of a game that reports runs, hits, and errors, and also the batteries for each team.

linesman: *Tennis:* An official who assists the referee by calling shots that fall out of bounds. *Ice Hockey:* Either of two officials who assist the referee and are chiefly responsible for calling offside and icing violations and conducting face-offs. *Soccer:* Either of two officials who assists the referee and is responsible for awarding goal kicks, corner kicks, and throw-ins. The linesman also marks where the ball goes out of bounds.

linkman: *Soccer:* A player, normally a halfback, who serves as a connecting element between the team's offensive and defensive players.

links: A golf course.

list: The tilt of a boat.

Little League Baseball (LLB): A private organization that promotes and supervises baseball programs for youngsters nine through 18 years of age. Little League games are played on a diamond that is two-thirds the size of the standard playing field.

lob: A ball hit or thrown in a slow, high arc. In tennis and other net games, the lob is an accepted piece of strategy against an opponent who comes to the net to volley.

loft: To hit a ball in a high arc. *Bowling:* To release a ball so that it hits down hard well beyond the foul line.

longbow: A wooden bow that is approximately five to six feet in length.

long jump: *Track and Field:* An event in which the competitor leaps for distance from a running start. Also called broad jump.

long relief man: *Baseball:* A relief pitcher who normally enters a game in the early innings, and thus pitches over a "long" distance.

look off: *Football:* The instance of a quarterback fooling or attempting to fool a defensive player by looking in one direction and then throwing a pass in the direction opposite.

loop drive: *Table Tennis:* A shot made with much topspin that just clears the net.

loose-ball foul: *Basketball:* In professional play, a foul committed by a player attempting to gain possession of a ball not under the control of either team.

losing pitcher: *Baseball, Softball:* The pitcher on a losing team who is charged with the loss.

lost ball: *Golf:* A ball not found after five minutes of searching. The penalty is one stroke.

love: *Tennis:* A score of zero.

low blow: *Boxing:* An illegal punch that lands below the belt.

low hurdles: *Track:* A race over hurdles 30 inches in height. Outdoor distances for such races are usually 180 yards (eight hurdles), 220 yards (10 hurdles), and 200 meters (10 hurdles).

luge: A one- or two-man wood or metal sled used for racing.

lure: *Fishing:* Artificial bait for catching fish.

M

magic number: In baseball, football, and other sports in which league championships are decided on a won-lost basis, the magic number is the combined total of wins for the league-leading team and losses for the second place team that will mathematically assure the league leader of the championship. For example, if Team A leads the league by seven games over Team B with 10 games remaining on the schedule, Team A's magic number is four.

maiden: *Horse Racing:* A racehorse that has never won a race.

mainmast: *Sailing:* The principal mast on a boat.

mainsail: *Sailing:* The principal sail on a boat.

major penalty: *Ice Hockey:* A penalty of five minutes called for fighting or some other infraction in which the referee judges there has been "intent to injure."

mallet: A long-handled implement with a cylinder-shaped head used to strike the ball in such sports as croquet and polo.

manager: A person in charge of the training and performance of an athlete or team. Also, in school or college sports, a student in charge of a team's equipment and records.

man in motion: *Football:* A player, normally a receiver, who turns and runs parallel to and just behind the line of scrimmage as the signals are being called, then breaks downfield just as the ball is snapped.

man-to-man defense: A defensive system common to basketball, ice hockey, and many other goal sports in which each member of a team on defense guards a particular member of the offensive team. Also called player-to-player defense. See zone defense.

marathon: A cross-country footrace of 26 miles, 385 yards.

mark: *Bowling:* A strike or a spare. *Track:* The starting line.

martial arts: The various branches of the Oriental combat sports, including karate, judo, jujitsu, kung fu, and sumo.

martingale: A part of a horse's harness designed to prevent the animal from throwing back its head.

massé: *Billiards, Pocket Billiards:* A stroke made by holding the cue almost straight up and down and hitting the cue ball on one side. The result is that the cue ball will curve around an obstructing ball to hit another.

mast: *Sailing:* A tall, vertical spar that rises directly from the keel to support sails.

Masters Tournament: An invitational golf tournament held at the Augusta (Georgia) National Golf Course each year since 1934.

match: Any contest or game in which two or more persons or teams oppose and compete with one another. *Tennis:* Competition based upon winning a specified number of sets, usually two sets out of three, or three sets out of five.

match penalty: *Ice Hockey:* A penalty in which a player is suspended for the remainder of the game. A match penalty is given for causing deliberate injury to an opponent.

match play: *Golf:* Competition in which scores are figured after each hole. The player or side taking the fewest strokes on the hole wins the hole. The player or side winning the most holes for the round wins the match. See stroke play.

match-up: The players who directly oppose one another in a game. In football, the wide receiver set to the right matches up against the strong safety.

mechanical bridge: *Billiards, Pocket Billiards:* A cue-like stick fitted with a small notched plate at the top end and used instead of a hand bridge when shooting over long distances.

medal play: *Golf:* See stroke play.

medicine ball: A large, heavy, leather ball tossed between individuals for exercise.

medley relay: *Swimming:* A relay race in which each member or team swims a different stroke for each leg. The backstroke is swum first, then the breast stroke, butterfly, and freestyle.

meet: A competition between two or more teams or clubs. Meet participants usually compete on an individual basis, but with their achievements counting toward a team point total or score.

metric mile: *Track:* A 1500-meter race. The term is derived from the fact that it is the metric race that is the closest equivalent to the mile.

midcourt line: *Basketball:* See division line.

middle guard: *Football:* The defensive lineman who is positioned between the tackles and opposite the offensive center. Also called nose guard.

middleweight: *Boxing:* A fighter weighing be-tween 147 and 160 pounds.

midfielder: *Soccer:* Any one of the three players who is positioned near the middle of the field between the forwards and backs.

mile relay: *Track:* A relay race in which each leg is one quarter of a mile long.

minor league: A league in professional sports made up of teams that are frequently owned by or in some way associated with major-league teams. The minor leagues often serve as training grounds for potential major-league players.

minor penalty: *Ice Hockey:* A penalty of two minutes given for such infractions as hooking, tripping, spearing, slashing, roughing, high-sticking, holding, elbowing, charging, or de-laying the game.

misconduct penalty: *Ice Hockey:* A penalty of 10 minutes for such infractions as extended fight-ing, abusive language, or failure to obey an official.

miscue: *Billiards, Pocket Billiards:* A faulty stroke that results when the cue tip slips from the cue ball.

miss: *Bowling:* To fail to convert a spare. Also called a blow. *Billiards, Pocket Billiards:* To fail to pocket or hit the intended object ball. A miss ends the player's inning.

mitt: A large, heavily padded, often circular glove worn by catchers in baseball and soft-ball. It usually consists of one section for the thumb and another section for the four fingers.

A mitt with less padding and constructed in two sections joined by leather webbing is worn by first basemen.

mixed doubles: In tennis and other court games, doubles play in which each side is made up of a man and woman.

mixed league: *Bowling:* A league in which teams are composed of both men and women.

mixed pairs: *Figure Skating:* Competition between teams consisting of a man and woman as dancing partners.

mixer: *Bowling:* A ball that causes the pins to bounce around.

mogul: A small mound of snow in a ski slope.

mohawk: *Figure Skating:* A turn from forward to backward (or backward to forward), from one foot to the other.

motorboat: See powerboat.

mound: *Baseball, Softball:* The elevated pitcher's area in the center of the diamond.

mountaineering: The sport of mountain climbing.

mousetrap: See trap block.

mouthpiece: A protective device made of rubber or plastic worn over the teeth by boxers and some football and hockey players. The mouthpiece helps to prevent cut lips and broken teeth.

mulligan: *Golf:* A free shot given a player after a poor one.

multiple foul: *Basketball:* The foul that results when two or more teammates commit personal fouls against the same player at approximately the same time. The fouled player receives a free throw for each foul.

multiple offense: *Football:* A type of attack based on the use of an assortment of formations.

N

National Association of Intercollegiate Athletics (NAIA): An organization that develops and sponsors athletic programs among colleges of small and moderate size.

National Basketball Association (NBA): An association of teams in professional basketball founded in 1946 as the Basketball Association of America. The present name was adopted in 1949.

National Football League (NFL): An association of teams in professional football, divided into the American Football Conference and National Football Conference. The champions of each conference face one another in the Super Bowl during January each year.

National Hockey League (NHL): An organization of professional hockey clubs representing principal cities in Canada and the United States.

National Invitational Tournament (NIT): A post-season college basketball tournament among specially invited teams held annually at Madison Square Garden in New York City since 1938.

National League (NL): An association of teams in professional baseball; one of baseball's two major leagues. The National League champion meets the American League champion in the World Series each fall.

National Rifle Association (NRA): An organization of target shooters, hunters, gun collectors, gunsmiths, law enforcement officials, and others interested in firearms.

net: A barrier of open-meshed cord or rope strung between two posts that divides a court in half, and over which a ball or shuttlecock must be hit in such games as tennis, table tennis, volleyball, and badminton.

net-cord shot: *Tennis:* A ball that skims the top of the net on any stroke except a serve and falls into the opponent's court. The opponent must play the ball as he would any shot that lands on his side of the net.

net-cord umpire: *Tennis:* An official stationed at one end of the net to detect serves that touch the net.

net game: *Tennis:* A style of play in which one stays close to the net in an attempt to volley.

neutral corner: *Boxing:* Either of two opposite corners of the ring not occupied by one of the boxers between rounds.

neutral position: *Figure Skating:* A position in which the arms, shoulders, and hips are square to the skater's line of travel.

neutral zone: *Ice Hockey:* The area on the ice between the two blue lines. Also called center ice. See defensive zone, attacking zone.

nine ball: A pocket billiards game played with balls numbered from one through nine. The balls must be pocketed in numerical order. The object of the game is to pocket the nine ball.

ninepins: An early bowling game in which nine bowling pins were arranged in a diamond shape as the target.

nock: *Archery:* The notch at the end of an arrow that fits onto the bowstring. Also, the grooves at either end of the bow for holding the bowstring.

nocking point: *Archery:* The point on the bowstring where the arrow is placed.

no-hitter: *Baseball, Softball:* A game in which one pitcher allows the opposing team no hits.

no man's land: In tennis and other net games, a midcourt area between the baseline and the service line from which it is difficult to make an effective return. The player is too far from the net to volley properly, and not back far enough to execute solid baseline strokes.

Nordic: *Skiing:* A class of skiing competition that includes both cross-country skiing and ski jumping. See cross-country skiing, Alpine.

North American Soccer League (NASL): An organization of professional soccer clubs representing more than 20 American and Canadian cities.

nose guard: See middle guard.

nose hit: *Bowling:* A hit square on the headpin.

numbering, numbering system: A system in the National Football League in which uniform numbers are assigned according to a player's position, as follows:

    1-19: quarterbacks and kickers
    20-49: running backs and defensive backs
    50-59: centers and linebackers
    60-79: defensive linemen and offensive
           linemen
    80-89: wide receivers and tight ends

nurse: *Billiards:* A playing technique in which the shooter keeps the balls in position for consecutive shots by striking them very softly.

O

oar: A long, thin wooden pole with a flat blade at one end, used to row and, occasionally, to steer a boat.

oarlock: A U-shaped metal frame mounted on the gunwale of a boat that serves as a resting place for the oar when rowing.

object ball: *Billiards, Pocket Billiards:* The ball a player wishes to hit or pocket with the cue ball.

odds: In betting, a ratio that expresses the probable outcome of an event. For example, the odds on a particular team may be two to one to win a specific game. This means that the bettor must risk one dollar for a chance to win two.

oddsmaker: A professional who sets odds for various sports events.

offense: A team or member of a team whose chief responsibility it is to attack and score points. Also, the technique or method of attack.

offensive backfield: *Football:* The players who line up behind the linemen and include the quarterback and the running backs.

offensive foul: *Basketball:* A personal foul committed by a player while his team has the ball. The penalty is loss of possession.

offensive holding: *Football:* Illegal use of the hands when blocking a defensive player. The penalty is 15 yards.

official: A person who supervises the play of a game or contest and administers the rules; a referee, an umpire.

off-season: The period of the year during which a particular sport is not played. The winter months are the traditional off-season for baseball.

offside, offsides: *Football:* For a player to be over the line of scrimmage before the ball is put in play. *Ice Hockey:* For a player to be illegally ahead of the puck in the attacking zone. *Soccer:* For a player to be in the attacking half of the field and illegally between the goal line and the ball.

off-speed pitch: *Baseball, Softball:* A pitch that is slower than normal.

Olympic Games: A program of amateur sports competition held every four years in a different country. The ancient Olympic Games were first celebrated in Greece in 776 B.C., and consisted of competition not only in athletics but in music, literature, and dance. The modern Olympic Games were first held in 1896. They offer competition in such sports as archery, basketball, boxing, canoeing, fencing, field hockey, gymnastics, ice hockey, judo, rowing, soccer, shooting, swimming and diving, track and field, water polo, weight lifting, wrestling, and yachting.

on deck: *Baseball, Softball:* Scheduled to bat after the present batter.

on-deck circle: *Baseball, Softball:* The chalked circle marked on each side of the playing field between the dugout and home plate, inside of which the next scheduled batter awaits his turn at the plate.

one-design: A class of racing sailboats with rigid design specifications.

one-on-one: A playground or schoolyard version of basketball between two players, one playing offense, the other defense. Only one half of the court and one basket is used.

one-two: *Boxing:* A combination of punches consisting of a left jab followed by a straight right.

on guard: *Fencing:* The basic starting position in which the fencer stands sideways to his opponent, the front foot pointing toward the opponent, the rear foot perpendicular to the front foot. The sword is pointed at the opponent and the left arm is partly extended to the rear.

onside: *Football:* Being on or behind the line of scrimmage. *Ice Hockey:* Being behind the puck when it is brought or passed into the attacking zone. *Soccer:* Being behind the ball when it is driven into the attacking half of the field.

onside kick: *Football:* A short kickoff by which the offensive team hopes to get possession of the ball. If the ball travels the legal minimum of 10 yards, it can be legally recovered by the kicking team.

open bowling: Non-tournament, non-league bowling; bowling for fun or practice.

open frame: *Bowling:* Any frame in which the bowler fails to register either a strike or spare.

open season: A period of the year when hunting is permitted for game or fish normally protected by law.

open stance: *Baseball, Softball:* A batter's position when awaiting the pitch in which the front foot is drawn farther back from the plate than the rear foot.

open tournament: A tournament that both amateurs and professionals may enter. Open tournaments are common to golf, tennis, and bowling.

optional: A routine of the competitor's own choosing. Gymnastics, diving, and figure skating are among the sports that permit optional (along with compulsory) routines.

option clause: A clause in a professional player's contract stating that the club has a claim on the player's services for one additional season following the date the contract expires. Thus, the option clause enables a team to lay claim to a player even though he has not agreed to a new contract. In professional football, the player becomes a free agent after the option year expires.

option play: *Football:* An offensive play in which the ballcarrier has the choice of running with the ball or passing it.

Orange Bowl: A postseason college football game played in Orange Bowl Stadium in Miami, Florida, between specially invited teams.

Oriental grip: *Table Tennis:* See penholder grip.

out: *Baseball, Softball:* The instance of retiring a batter or base runner by the team in the field. A team is out when three of its players have been retired in the same inning.

outboard motor: A detachable motor that is mounted in the stern of a boat.

outfield: *Baseball, Softball:* The playing area that extends outward from the infield between the foul lines, divided into right, center, and left field.

outfielder: *Baseball, Softball:* The members of a team that play the outfield, the right fielder, center fielder, and left fielder.

outlet pass: *Basketball:* A pass used by a team to trigger a fast break following a rebound or a steal.

out of bounds: On or over the sidelines or end-lines of a field or court.

out-of-bounds play: *Basketball:* A play used by a team in possession of the ball out of bounds that is meant to free a player to receive the throw in.

outside: *Football:* Toward the sideline.

outside edge: *Figure Skating:* The right edge of the right skate; the left edge of the left skate.

outside forward: *Soccer:* Either of the two members of the forward line who play along the sides of the field.

outside half: *Soccer:* Either of the two halfbacks who normally play near the sides of the field.

over grip: See regular grip.

overhand: A stroke in which the paddle or racket is brought down rapidly and forcefully on a ball. Also, a throw in which the hand comes forward and down from above shoulder level.

overhead kick: See scissors kick.

overlapping grip: See Vardon grip.

over play: To guard an opponent more toward his more effective hand or side in an effort to force him to use the other hand or side.

overspin: See topspin.

overtime: An extension of playing time beyond the established limit to decide the winner of a contest when the score is tied. In basketball, the overtime period is five minutes in length. In professional football, an overtime period is a maximum of 15 minutes in length; it ends when one side scores. In ice hockey, the overtime period is a maximum of 5 minutes in length; it ends when one team scores. In volleyball, play continues until one side has gained a two-point advantage.

P

pace: The rate of speed at which a person or animal walks or runs. Also, the gait of a pacing horse. See pacer.

pace car: *Auto Racing:* The automobile that leads the field of competitors through the warm-up laps, then pulls off the course just before the race begins.

pacemaker: One who sets the pace in a race.

pacer: *Harness Racing:* A standardbred whose gait is a pace, that is, a horse in which both feet on the one side leave and return to the ground together. See trotter.

packed powder: *Skiing:* Snow that is packed down but not icy.

paddle: A wooden implement with a blade at one end that is used without an oarlock to propel a canoe or small boat.

paddleball: A game played under the rules of handball, except that the players are equipped with paddles.

paddleboard: See kickboard.

paddle tennis: A scaled-down version of tennis played with wooden paddles and a deadened tennis ball on a cement or asphalt court. Also called playground paddle tennis.

paddock: *Horse Racing:* The area of a track where the horses are saddled and paraded before a race.

pair skating: *Figure Skating:* Competition involving various lifts, spins, and free-style movements performed by a man and a woman simultaneously and in harmony.

palming: *Basketball:* A violation of the rules in which the ball, while it is being dribbled, is allowed to rest momentarily in the upturned palm. The penalty is loss of possession.

Pan-American Games: A program of amateur sports competition among nations of the Western Hemisphere held every four years since 1951.

par: *Golf:* The number of strokes an expert player would be expected to make on a given hole.

parallel bars: *Gymnastics:* A pair of wooden bars approximately 11½ feet in length and 16 inches apart that are mounted five and a half feet above the floor. The bars are used to perform various swinging and balancing stunts in men's gymnastics.

parallel turn: *Skiing:* A turn executed with the skis parallel throughout.

parry: In boxing and fencing, to ward off or deflect a blow or thrust.

pass: *Baseball, Softball:* See base on balls.

passed ball: *Baseball, Softball:* A pitch missed by the catcher and that enables a base runner to advance.

pass pattern: *Football:* The specific route run by a pass receiver in moving downfield to catch a pass.

pass rush: *Football:* The effort on the part of the defensive linemen to deck the quarterback or otherwise interfere with his effort to pass the ball.

patch: *Figure Skating:* A space on the ice rented by a skater to practice figures.

patch marker: *Figure Skating:* A device used to inscribe loops, circles, and other figures within a patch. Once marked on the ice, a figure is traced and retraced by the skater as a training exercise.

pattern: See pass pattern.

penalize: To punish an individual or team by means of a penalty.

penalty: The punishment imposed upon an individual or team for breaking a rule. Penalties vary, depending on the sport. In basketball, a team can be penalized by being made to lose possession of the ball or by the awarding of foul shots to the offended player. In football, a team is penalized by losing yardage. In golf, one stroke or two strokes may be added to the golfer's score. In ice hockey, a penalized player is suspended from the game for a certain number of minutes. To penalize a soccer team, a free kick is awarded the opposition.

penalty area: *Soccer:* The rectangular-shaped area at each end of the field which measures 18 yards by 44 yards. Penalty kicks are taken from within the penalty area.

penalty box: *Ice Hockey:* A bench alongside the ice where penalized players must remain for the duration of their penalties. Also called the sin bin.

penalty kick: *Soccer:* A direct free kick awarded a team when the opposing team commits a major foul within the penalty area. Only the goalie is permitted to defend against the kick. See direct free kick.

penalty killer: *Ice Hockey:* A player who is sent out onto the ice when his team is playing short-handed because of a penalty, and whose ability as a skater, stickhandler, and passer enables him to keep control of the puck while the penalty minutes are consumed. Penalty killers frequently work in pairs.

penalty shot: *Ice Hockey:* A free shot at the goal with only the goalie permitted to block the puck.

penholder grip: *Table Tennis:* A method of gripping the paddle in which the face of the paddle is pointed downward and the handle grasped between the thumb and forefinger. The other three fingers support the paddle from behind. Also called the Oriental grip.

pennant: *Baseball:* The league championship.

pentathlon: An athletic contest in which each contestant participates in five different track and field events: the long jump, high jump,

200-meter dash, discus throw, and one-mile run. Points are awarded on the basis of each athlete's performance in each event, and the winner is the contestant with the highest point total.

perfect game: *Baseball, Softball:* A no-hitter in which not one opposing batter is permitted to reach first base. *Bowling:* A game of 12 consecutive strikes; a 300 game.

period: A division of playing time in a game. In football, a period is the same as a quarter. In ice hockey, a period is one of the game's three 20-minute segments of play.

personal foul: *Basketball:* An infraction that involves illegal physical contact with another player. The player fouled may be awarded one or two free throws, or his team may be given possession of the ball, depending upon the circumstances of the foul.

photo finish: A race in which the leading competitors cross the finish line so closely together that the winner can only be determined by a photograph taken at the instant the line is crossed.

pick: *Basketball:* A screen play in which the player with the ball, instead of shooting, drives for the basket and attempts a lay-up. See screen play. *Figure Skating:* See toe pick.

pick-and-roll: *Basketball:* A play in which the player setting a screen for a teammate with the ball suddenly cuts toward the basket for a pass. See screen play.

picket fence: *Bowling:* A leave in which the 1, 2, 4, and 7 pins, or the 1, 3, 6, and 10 pins, are left standing.

pick off: *Baseball, Softball:* To catch a runner off base, usually by virtue of a sudden throw by either the pitcher or catcher.

pigeon: *Skeet, Trapshooting:* See clay pigeon.

pigskin: A football.

pike: A body position common to diving and gymnastics in which the body is bent at the waist, the legs are held straight, and the hands reach forward to touch the feet.

piling on: *Football:* The action of one or more defensive players who jump on the ballcarrier after he has been tackled. Piling on is illegal; the penalty is 15 yards.

pin: *Wrestling:* To force an opponent's shoulder to the mat. *Golf:* The slim pole to which the pennant that marks the hole is secured. *Bowling:* See bowling pin.

pin bowling: Aiming the ball directly at the pins instead of a target on the lane. See spot bowling.

pinch hit: *Baseball, Softball:* To bat in place of a player who is scheduled to bat.

pinch-hitter: *Baseball, Softball:* A player who enters the game to bat in place of another player.

pinch-runner: *Baseball, Softball:* A player who is sent into the game to run for another player.

pin deck: *Bowling:* The section of the alley where the pins are spotted.

pinfall: *Bowling:* The number of pins a bowler knocks down with one ball, in a frame, for a game, or for a series of games.

Ping Pong: See table tennis.

pinsetter, pinspotter: *Bowling:* The automatic machine that sets up the pins.

pistol: A small, short gun held and fired with one hand.

pit: *Auto Racing:* An area alongside the race course where vehicles are refueled and repaired. *Bowling:* The area at the far end of the alley into which toppled pins fall. *Track and Field:* The landing area for such events as the long jump and pole vault.

pitch-and-run: See chip shot.

pitcher: *Baseball, Softball:* The player who delivers the ball to the hitter.

pitcher's mound: *Baseball:* The elevated portion of the playing field on a line between home plate and second base. The rules permit a pitcher's mound to be as high as 10 inches.

pitcher's rubber: See rubber.

pitchout: *Baseball:* A pitch deliberately thrown high and wide to the batter to make it easier for the catcher to attempt a pick-off or throw out a runner attempting to steal. *Football:* A lateral pass, usually from the quarterback to a running back.

pitch shot: *Golf:* A short, lofted shot that is usually hit with backspin.

piton: *Mountain Climbing:* A metal spike which is driven into a crack in a rock face, and that is fitted with an eye or ring through which a rope can be passed to aid the climber in ascending or descending.

pivot, pivotman: *Basketball:* The player who stations himself at either side of or near the top of the free-throw lane, and who serves as a focal point for the offense with his passing, screening, and shooting.

place: *Horse Racing:* To finish second.

place kick: *Football:* A kick for which the ball is held in a fixed position. A place kick is used to put the ball in play after a touchdown, and when attempting a field goal or the point after touchdown.

plate: See home plate.

platform: *Diving:* A flat and rigid surface, approximately 20 feet long and six feet wide and 10 meters above the water, from which divers leap in competition.

platform tennis: A variation of tennis played on a wooden or aluminum platform that is enclosed by a high, taut wire screen with participants using wooden paddles and a sponge-rubber ball.

play-action pass: *Football:* A pass play in which the quarterback first fakes a handoff to a running back.

playbook: *Football:* A usually spiral-bound, three-hole notebook which contains a team's formations, plays, and a vocabulary of the technical terms it uses. A playbook is issued to each member of the team at the beginning of the training season.

player-to-player defense: See man-to-man defense.

playground ball: An inflated rubber ball about the size of a basketball that is used in playing a variety of schoolyard or playground ball games.

playground paddle tennis: See paddle tennis.

playmaker: A member of a team in basketball, ice hockey, and other goal games who is skilled in creating scoring opportunities for the team.

play through: *Golf:* The instance of one group of players moving ahead of a slower group.

poach: In doubles play in tennis and other court games, to cross into one's partner's court to cut off a shot and volley.

pocket: *Football:* A protected area formed by members of the offensive line several yards behind the line of scrimmage within which the quarterback sets up to pass. *Bowling:* The space between the 1 pin and the 3 pin (for right-handers) which serves as the bowler's target when aiming for a strike. *Pocket Billiards:* Any one of the six openings on the table into which the balls are hit. *Baseball:* The part of a glove or mitt in which the ball is caught.

pocket billiards: Any of several games played on a rectangular cloth-covered six-pocket table with raised cushioned edges, using a long, tapering cue, a white cue ball, and 15 colored balls numbered from one to 15. The object of the game is to drive the cue ball into an object ball, sending it into a pocket. Also called pool. See eight ball, rotation, and straight pool.

point: The unit of scoring in most games.

point after touchdown: *Football:* The single point added to a team's score by making a successful place kick over the crossbar. A team must first score a touchdown to be given the opportunity to try for the point. Also called conversion, extra point.

pointer: One of a breed of hunting dogs that tracks down game by scent and shows where the game is to be found by standing still with its head pointing toward it.

point guard: *Basketball:* A guard who acts as the team's chief ballhandler. See playmaker.

point man: *Ice Hockey:* A defenseman who takes up a position on either side of the ice just inside the attacking zone when his team is on the attack. From his point position, the player backs up the play of the forward on his side of the rink, helping to keep the puck in the attacking zone.

point spread: The number of points by which a stronger team can be expected to defeat a weaker team.

poison ivy: *Bowling:* The 3-6-10 split.

poke check: *Ice Hockey:* A quick thrust with the stick blade in an attempt to knock the puck away from an opponent.

pole position: *Auto Racing:* At the start of a race, the position on the inside of the front row.

pole vault: *Track and Field:* A field event in which each competitor uses a long pole to spring his body over a high crossbar.

polo: A game played on horseback by two teams of four players, each of whom is equipped with a long-handled mallet for driving a small wooden ball through the opponent's goal.

pomalift: *Skiing:* A lift that consists of a disc-shaped seat that is connected by a metal rod or bar to a moving overhead cable. The skier leans against the seat to be towed up the hill.

pommel: The raised front portion of a saddle. *Gymnastics:* Either of two hand grips fixed to the top of the pommel horse.

pommel horse: *Gymnastics:* A piece of equipment in men's gymnastics that consists of an upholstered body about five feet long and one foot wide, and with its top surface approximately three and a quarter feet above the floor. Two pommels are fixed to the top of the horse about 16 inches apart. The pommel horse is used in performing a variety of vaulting exercises.

pool: See pocket billiards.

pop fly: *Baseball, Softball:* A short, high fly ball, usually caught by an infielder.

pop out, pop up: *Baseball, Softball:* To hit a pop fly that is caught for an out.

port: *Boating:* The left side of a boat when one faces forward.

position play: *Billiards, Pocket Billiards:* A basic method of play in which the cue ball is struck in such a way that it ends up in the right spot for the next shot.

post: *Basketball:* An offensive position on the court to the right or left of the free-throw lane. Usually it's the team's center that occupies the post. *Football:* A pass route in which the receiver races downfield, veering toward the center of the field and the goalposts. *Horse Racing:* The starting gate at a race track.

powder: *Skiing:* Light, dry, fine snow.

powder puff: *Bowling:* A ball that rolls without either power or speed.

powerboat: A boat propelled by either an inboard or outboard engine. Also called a motorboat.

power forward: *Basketball:* A forward who not only is a top scorer, but also plays the pivot, rebounds, and blocks shots.

power play: *Ice Hockey:* A play that results when one team has a numerical advantage in players over the opposing team because of penalties. In executing a power play, the team with the advantage normally sends five men with the puck into the penalized team's defensive zone.

power sweep: See sweep.

press: *Basketball:* A defensive tactic in which players guard their opponents tightly, attempting to disrupt the team's effort to pass and dribble, the idea being to get possession of the ball. The press is often used in the closing minutes of a game by a team that is trailing. *Weight Lifting:* A lift in which the weight is thrust from shoulder level to a position straight overhead solely by straightening the arms; there can be no movement of the feet or legs.

primary receiver: *Football:* The player who is designated to receive the ball by the quarterback in the huddle.

prize fight: A match between professional boxers for money.

professional: A person who makes his or her living as an athlete.

prone float: See dead-man's float.

puck: *Ice Hockey:* The hard rubber disc three inches in diameter and one inch thick, and weighing about six ounces, that is used as a playing medium instead of a ball.

puck-carrier: *Ice Hockey:* The player who has the puck in his possession.

pull: *Baseball, Softball:* To hit a ball in the direction one is facing when the swing is completed. Thus, a right-handed batter, who stands on the left side of home plate and faces left at the end of the swing, will pull the ball toward left field. *Football:* The action of an offensive lineman, usually a guard but occasionally a tackle, who steps back from his position in the line, then quickly turns and dashes to one side to lead the ballcarrier.

pump: To use the ball to fake a forward pass (in football) or a shot (in basketball).

punch: A sharp blow with the fists. *Baseball, Softball:* to hit the ball with less than a full swing.

punchball: A variation of baseball common to playgrounds and schoolyards. Instead of a baseball being hit with a bat, an inflated rubber ball is punched with the fist.

punching bag: See speed bag.

punt: *Football:* A kick in which the ball is dropped from the hands and kicked with the instep before it reaches the ground. Punts usually occur when it is fourth down for a team that does not want to risk losing possession by trying for a first down, but is too far away from the opponent's goal line to attempt a field goal.

punter: *Football:* A player who specializes in punting.

punt return: *Football:* The runback of a punted ball.

push-up: A conditioning exercise performed by lying prone and pushing the body off the floor by straightening the arms, then lowering the body until the chest touches the floor. The exercise is then repeated a specific number of times.

putout: *Baseball, Softball:* A play in which a batter or base runner is retired. The ways in which a batter can be put out include striking out, hitting a fly ball that is caught, being tagged with the ball while off base, or being forced to advance to a base that is touched by a player with the ball.

putt: *Golf:* A light stroke made on the putting green or from just off the green using a putter in an effort to put the ball in the hole.

putter: *Golf:* A short club with a flat face used for putting.

putting green: *Golf:* The smooth, closely-cropped grassy plot that contains the hole into which the ball must be played. All strokes on the putting green must be made with the putter.

Q

quarter: One of four equal periods of playing time in which some games are divided.

quarterback: *Football:* The backfield player who receives the ball from the center on most offensive plays. The quarterback calls signals, throws forward passes, may run with the ball occasionally, and in general, directs the team's attack.

quarterback sneak: *Football:* An offensive play in which the quarterback upon receiving the ball from the center plunges into the line, with the center and guards blocking for him.

quarterfinals: In an elimination tournament, the round before the semifinal round. See semifinal.

quarterhorse: One of a breed of horses developed in the western United States and originally trained for races up to a quarter of a mile.

Queensberry rules: A boxing code of fair play devised in England in 1869 by the Marquis of Queensberry, and which serves as the basic rules under which matches are conducted today.

quick count: *Football:* The instance of a quarterback calling the signals at the line of scrimmage at a faster than normal pace in an effort to take the defensive team by surprise.

quick kick: *Football:* A surprise punt.

quiver: *Archery:* A portable case for carrying arrows.

R

rabbit ball: *Baseball:* A baseball that is livelier than normal, and thus one capable of being hit a long distance.

rabbit punch: *Boxing:* An illegal blow to the back of the head.

race-walk: *Track and Field:* A race in which competitors are limited to using a fast walk. Continuous contact with the ground must be maintained; a competitor is not permitted to raise one foot until the heel of the other foot touches the ground.

racing dive: *Swimming:* A flat, shallow dive that is executed from the starting platform at the beginning of a race.

rack: *Pocket Billiards:* The wooden or plastic triangle used to position the balls at the beginning of a game.

racquet, racket: The implement used to hit the ball or shuttlecock in various net or wall games, such as tennis, squash, and badminton. Usually made of wood or lightweight metal, a racket consists of a handle with a round or oval frame at one end which is strung with catgut or nylon to provide the hitting surface.

racquetball: A game played on a four-walled handball court using the same rules as in handball, except that a racquet is used to hit the ball.

racquets: A game played on a large four-walled court that is much the same as squash racquets, the principal difference being that only the side that serves can score points. See squash racquets.

railroad: *Bowling:* Any difficult split, such as the 7-10, 8-10, or 4-6.

rain check: A ticket stub for a baseball game or other outdoor sports event that entitles the holder to admission to another contest if the original game or event is canceled because of rain.

rally: In tennis, handball, badminton, and other court games, to hit the ball back and forth in practice or in the course of playing a point. In baseball, ice hockey, soccer, and other team sports, a rally is any sudden scoring outburst, especially one that takes place late in the game by a team that is trailing. In automobile and motorcycle racing, a rally is a race that is usually run over public roads under prevailing traffic conditions between checkpoints that are announced just before the start.

rangefinder: *Bowling:* Any of the seven small triangles embedded in the lane 12 to 16 feet beyond the foul line, used as targets in spot bowling. See spot bowling.

rattle: To fluster or unnerve an opponent by persistent needling.

RBI: *Baseball, Softball:* A run batted in.

reach: *Sailing:* To sail a course that is approximately at right angles to the wind.

ready list: *Football:* A selection of 20 to 30 plays a team plans to use against a particular opponent.

rebound: *Basketball:* A missed shot that bounces off the backboard or the rim. *Ice Hockey:* A missed shot that hits the goal or goalkeeper and bounces away.

rebounder: *Basketball:* A player noted for his ability in recovering rebounds.

receiver: *Football:* An offensive player who is eligible to receive a forward pass. Running backs and wide receivers are the normal receivers. *Tennis:* The player who receives the serve. *Track:* In a relay race, the player who receives the baton during an exchange. *Baseball, Softball:* The catcher.

reception: *Football:* A forward pass that is caught by a receiver; also called a completion.

record: The best performance known; also, information or data that is collected concerning an individual, team, or league.

recover: To gain possession of a loose ball or puck.

recurved bow: *Archery:* A bow that is formed in such a way that its tips form reverse curves.

red card: *Soccer:* The red card, about the size of an ordinary playing card, that is shown by the referee to indicate a player is being sent off the field for a violation of the rules.

red dog: *Football:* See blitz.

red flag: *Auto Racing:* The solid red flag that is displayed to signal that a race is being halted and all drivers must immediately stop.

red light: *Ice Hockey:* The red light behind each of the goals that is lighted by the goal judge to indicate that a goal has been scored.

red line: *Ice Hockey:* The one-foot-wide red line that divides the rink into halves and serves to indicate offside and icing violations.

reef: *Sailing:* To reduce the size of a sail by rilling or tucking a part of it and tying it to a mast or spar.

reel: *Fishing:* A metal spool that is enclosed within a frame and that is attached to the butt end of the rod and is used to let out or wind up the line.

referee: The official who supervises the play of a game or contest.

referee's crease: *Ice Hockey:* A semicircle with a radius of 10 feet that is located directly in front of the timekeeper's desk. Only the referee is permitted to enter the crease.

regatta: A boat race or an organized series of boat races.

regular grip: *Gymnastics:* A method of grasping a horizontal bar in which the palms face away from the body as the grip is taken. Also called front grip, over grip.

regulator: *Scuba Diving:* A device that provides the diver with air from his air tank when he demands it, that is, when he inhales, and at a pressure that is equal to that of the surrounding water.

reins: *Horseback Riding:* The long, narrow leather straps attached to the bit in a horse's mouth and used by the rider to control the animal.

relay, relay race: In track and swimming, a race between two or more teams in which each team member runs only a set part of the race (called a leg), and is then relieved by another member of the team. Relay races frequently consist of four legs, and are often conducted at distances of 400 to 800 meters or 440 to 880 yards.

relief pitcher, reliever: *Baseball, Softball:* A pitcher called into a game to replace another pitcher.

resin bag: See rosin bag.

restraining circle: *Basketball:* One of the three 12-foot circles on the basketball court within which jump ball plays are conducted. Only the two players jumping are permitted to enter the circle.

retire: *Baseball, Softball:* To put out a batter or base runner.

retriever: Any of several breeds of medium-size hunting dogs developed and trained to seek out and bring back game shot by the hunter.

returner: *Football:* A player who is assigned to run back punts and kickoffs.

Reuther board: *Gymnastics:* See beat board.

rev counter: *Auto Racing:* See tachometer.

reverse: *Football:* An offensive play in which a ballcarrier who is running toward one side of the field hands the ball to a teammate who is running in the opposite direction.

reverse grip: *Gymnastics:* A method of gripping a horizontal bar in which the palms face toward the body as the grip is taken. Also called under grip.

revolver: A pistol that can be fired several times without being loaded again. See pistol.

rifle: A gun with spiral grooves in its barrel which spins the bullet as it is shot.

right field: *Baseball, Softball:* The right side of the outfield as viewed from home plate; the outfield area beyond first base.

right fielder: *Baseball, Softball:* The player who plays right field.

rim: *Basketball:* The circular metal ring 18 inches in diameter from which the net is hung.

ring: *Boxing:* An area that is usually about 20 feet square and is enclosed by three parallel ropes within which a bout is conducted.

ringer: A contestant entered dishonestly into a race or contest. Also, a horseshoe that is thrown to encircle the stake and is worth three points.

rings: *Gymnastics:* A pair of metal or wooden rings approximately nine inches in diameter that are suspended from the ceiling by ropes to hang about eight feet from the floor and 20 inches apart. The rings are used in men's competition in performing various swinging and balancing movements.

rink: An area with a surface of smooth ice for skating. Also, a smooth floor for roller skating.

rip cord: *Sky Diving:* The cord pulled to release the parachute.

riposte: *Fencing:* A quick thrust given immediately following a successful parry.

road course: *Auto Racing:* A race course laid out over public roads or a course designed and constructed to simulate public roads, with hills, sharp curves, and right and left turns.

road race: *Cycling:* A race at a distance of from 10 to 100 miles over public roads, usually involving teams of riders. *Auto Racing:* A race conducted on a road course over a fixed distance. It can also be conducted for a fixed period of time; the winner is the competitor covering the greatest distance in that time.

road rash: *Roller Skating, In-line Skating, Cycling, Skateboarding:* What can occur on parts of the body after a fall.

rocker: The curve along the bottom of an ice-skate blade.

rodeo: Competition for public entertainment involving skills important to cowboys of the western United States and Canada. Rodeo events include calf roping, steer wrestling, steer roping, bareback riding, and saddle bronc riding.

roll, roll out: *Football:* To move to the right or left with the ball before throwing a pass or tossing a lateral. Usually it's the quarterback who rolls out.

roll bar: *Auto Racing:* A steel bar mounted to the car frame that curves over the driver's head and helps to protect him should the car turn over.

roller derby: Speed skating on roller skates around a banked oval track between professional teams of men and women, 10 skaters to a team. Points are given when an individual skater breaks away from the pack to circle the track and lap opposing skaters.

roller hockey: A version of ice hockey played on city streets and in parks and playgrounds by players who wear roller skates and use hockey sticks.

roller skate: A skate with two pairs of wheels mounted to the sole, one pair behind the other.

Rose Bowl: A postseason college football game played in the Rose Bowl Stadium in Pasadena, California. The first Rose Bowl Game was played in 1902. In recent years, the game has matched teams representing the Pacific-10 Conference and Big-10 Conference.

rosin bag: *Baseball, Softball:* A small cloth bag filled with powdered rosin used by the pitcher to increase the friction of the fingers when gripping the ball. Also called resin bag.

roster: A list of members of a team.

rotation: A pocket billiards game in which the balls are played in numerical order, with points awarded according to the number of each ball pocketed.

rouge: In Canadian football, the one point the kicking team receives when a punt or missed field goal goes out of bounds beyond the field's end line, or when a punt or missed field goal is recovered by a defensive player who is then tackled in the end zone.

rough: *Golf:* That part of the course left unmowed and untrimmed.

roughing the kicker: *Football:* A personal foul that is called when a defensive player runs into or knocks down the punter without touching the ball. The penalty is 15 yards from where the ball was spotted on the previous play.

roughing the passer: *Football:* A personal foul that is called when a defensive player runs into or tackles the quarterback after a forward pass has been thrown. The penalty is 15 yards from where the ball was spotted on the previous play.

round: *Boxing:* One of the periods of boxing into which a bout is divided. In professional boxing, a round lasts three minutes with a one-minute interval between rounds. *Archery:* An event in which each contestant shoots a specified number of arrows at a specified distance from the target. *Golf:* A complete circuit of the course, normally consisting of 18 holes.

roundball: The game of basketball.

roundhouse: *Boxing:* A blow delivered with a wide swing.

round off: *Gymnastics:* A stunt similar to the cartwheel, but which includes a handstand and a quarter turn of the body.

round robin: A tournament in which each contestant is matched against every other contestant.

round-tripper: *Baseball, Softball:* A home run.

rubber: *Baseball, Softball:* The oblong piece of hard rubber set crosswise in the pitcher's mound. The pitcher must stay in contact with the rubber as he delivers the ball. Also called pitcher's rubber.

rucksack: A canvas backpack designed to be worn without a pack frame.

rudder: A hinged plate of metal or wood attached to the stern of a boat beneath the water line that is used to control the direction of the boat. When the rudder is turned in one direction, it forces the bow of the boat to move in that direction.

rugby, rugby football: A form of football played with an inflated oval ball on a large rectangular field between two teams of 15 players. The object is to kick or carry the ball over the opposition goal line. Forward passing, substitution of players, and time-outs are not permitted.

rugger: The game of rugby.

run: *Baseball, Softball:* The point scored by running from home plate around the bases and back to home plate. *Football:* A play in which a player attempts to carry the ball past or through an opposing team. *Billiards, Pocket Billiards:* A series of consecutive scoring shots. *Skiing, Bobsledding:* A downhill course.

run and hit: *Baseball, Softball:* A play in which a runner breaks for second base as the pitch is delivered. It is similar to the hit-and-run play, except that the batter is not required to try to hit the pitch. See hit and run.

runback: *Football:* The act of returning a punt, kickoff, or intercepted forward pass.

run batted in: *Baseball, Softball:* A run that scores as the result of a base hit or some other offensive action on the part of the batter.

rundown: *Baseball, Softball:* A play in which a base runner is trapped between two bases and is tagged out. Often the ball will be thrown back and forth several times from one infield to another before the tag is made.

running back: *Football:* A member of the offensive backfield who is used to carry the ball on running plays or is assigned to block.

running high jump: *Track and Field:* An event in which competitors jump for height over an adjustable crossbar, each taking a preliminary run to the take-off point.

running lane: *Bowling:* An alley on which the ball hooks easily.

running long jump, running broad jump: *Track and Field:* An event in which competitors leap for distance, with each taking a preliminary run to their take-off point.

runway: *Bowling:* See approach.

rush: *Football:* To move the ball by running instead of passing.

S

saber: *Fencing:* A heavy sword with two cutting edges.

sack: *Baseball, Softball:* A base. *Football:* To tackle the quarterback behind the line of scrimmage before a forward pass can be thrown.

sacrifice fly: *Baseball, Softball:* A fair or foul hit with less than two out that is caught for an out, after which a runner tags up and advances a base. It does not count as a time at bat.

sacrifice hit: *Baseball, Softball:* A bunt made with less than two out that advances a base runner and on which the batter is put out. A sacrifice hit does not count as a time at bat for the batter; thus, it does not affect one's batting average.

saddle: A leather seat placed on the back of a horse for riding; also a bicycle seat.

saddle bronc riding: *Rodeo:* An event in which contestants are required to ride a saddled wild horse for 10 seconds.

saddle cloth: *Horse Racing:* The cloth placed under the saddle which bears the horse's number.

safe: *Baseball, Softball:* To reach a base without being put out.

safety: *Baseball, Softball:* A base hit. *Billiards, Pool:* A stroke in which the player does not attempt to score, but rather to leave the cue ball in such a position that his opponent is faced with a difficult or impossible shot. *Football:* A play in which the ballcarrier is tackled in his own end zone; two points are credited to the defensive team; also, either one of the two defensive players who line up farthest from the line of scrimmage. *Hunting:* A device on a gun that locks the trigger and prevents it from being fired accidentally.

safety blitz: *Football:* An all-out charge by one or both of the safeties in an effort to spill the quarterback.

safety valve: *Football:* A short pass thrown to a running back when the wide receivers are covered.

sag, sagging: *Basketball:* A type of defense in which one or more players drops off the opponent being covered to guard a player nearer to the basket. Also called collapsing defense.

sail: A piece of material, usually triangular in shape, that catches the wind to propel a boat.

sailboat: A boat with sails; thus, one powered by the wind.

sailplane: A type of glider which is capable of soaring to an altitude higher than its take-off point.

Salchow: *Figure Skating:* A jump from the inside back edge of one foot, followed by a full turn in the air, landing on the outside back edge of the other foot.

salto: *Gymnastics:* A forward or backward somersault performed in the air.

sandbagger: *Bowling:* An individual who purposely keeps down his average in order to receive a higher handicap than he deserves.

sand trap: *Golf:* A depression on the course that is filled with sand and that is meant to offer a difficult challenge to the golfer.

sand wedge: *Golf:* An iron golf club used in getting a ball out of a sand trap.

save: *Baseball:* The credit given a relief pitcher who enters the game with his or her team in the lead and preserves the lead for the remainder of the game. *Field Hockey, Ice Hockey, Lacrosse, Soccer:* To block the ball or puck from entering the net, thereby preventing a goal from being scored.

scale: *Gymnastics:* A balanced position in which one stands on one foot with the free leg extended out and up to the rear or side.

scalper: An individual who sells tickets for an event at a price higher than their established value.

school figures: *Figure Skating:* A group of specific movements and patterns that are required to be skated in official competition.

schuss: *Skiing:* A straight, downhill run.

scissors kick: *Swimming:* A kick in which the legs are moved apart to a stride position, then brought together again forcefully. *Soccer:* A kick executed by jumping up and kicking the ball back over one's head with a scissors movement of the legs.

scout: A person employed to gather information about an individual athlete or team.

scouting: The practice of observing the performances of individual athletes in order to evaluate their abilities. Also, observing the play of a future opposing team to determine its strengths and weaknesses.

scramble: *Football:* The effort of a quarterback who runs around behind the line of scrimmage in an effort to elude would-be tacklers.

scrambler: *Football:* A quarterback with a reputation for scrambling.

scratch: *Horse Racing:* To withdraw a horse from a race. *Pocket Billiards:* Any shot that results in a penalty, as when the cue ball is pocketed.

scratch hit: *Baseball:* A batted ball that is not solidly struck, but which results in a base hit.

screen: *Basketball:* A move in which an offensive player positions his or her body so that it acts as a barrier. From behind the barrier, a teammate is free to shoot the ball.

screen pass: *Football:* A short forward pass either to the right or left to a running back in front of whom a wall of blockers has formed.

screen play: *Basketball:* An offensive maneuver in which one player shoots while a second player blocks off a close defender.

screen shot: *Ice Hockey:* A shot taken while one or more players obstructs the goalie's view of the puck.

screwball: *Baseball:* A pitch that breaks toward a right-handed batter if delivered by a right-handed pitcher.

scrimmage: *Football:* The contest between two opposing teams that begins at the time the ball is snapped until it is out of play; also, a practice game, often between teams formed from the same squad of players.

scrum: *Rugby:* A formation in which opposing players mass together around the ball and, with their heads down, attempt to shoulder their opponents out of the way and kick the ball to a member of their own team.

scrummage: See scrum.

scuba: An equipment system that includes an air tank, hoses, a mouthpiece, and regulating device which permits underwater breathing. The word is an acronym for *self-contained under-water breathing apparatus*.

scull: To propel a boat by means of an oar mounted in the stern.

seam: *Basketball, Football:* An open area between two zones of coverage in a zone defense.

seat: *Horseback Riding:* The rider's position in the saddle.

second: *Boxing:* An individual who advises and aids a boxer between rounds during a bout.

secondary: *Football:* The four players — the two safeties and two cornerbacks — who make up a team's defensive backfield.

second base: *Baseball, Softball:* The base across the diamond from home plate.

second baseman: *Baseball, Softball:* The infielder who is assigned to play to the right of second base and is responsible, with the shortstop, for covering second base.

second sacker: *Baseball:* The second baseman.

second-string player: A substitute.

seed: *Tennis, Ping Pong, Badminton:* To schedule players or teams in a tournament so that the better ones will not be matched in the early rounds.

semifinal: In an elimination tournament, the round just before the final round.

semi fingertip grip: *Bowling:* A grip in which the fingers are inserted into the holes up to a point midway between the first and second joints, while the thumb is inserted to the normal depth, up to the second joint. See conventional grip, fingertip grip.

serve: To put the ball in play. In tennis and other racket games, one serves by hitting over a net. In handball, the serve is against a wall.

service ace: *Tennis, Handball:* A serve that one's opponent cannot touch and which counts as a score for the server.

service break: *Tennis:* The instance of a player winning a game against an opponent's serve.

service line: *Tennis:* The line 21 feet from the net in each player's court that marks the rear boundary of the service boxes.

set: *Tennis:* The scoring unit between the game and match. The individual or team that wins at least six games by a margin of two games wins the set.The outcome of a match is determined by the number of sets won, as two sets out of three.

set point: *Tennis:* A situation in which an individual or team can win the set by winning the next point.

set position: *Baseball:* The position of the pitcher as he checks the base runner. One foot is in contact with the pitcher's rubber; he holds the ball in front of his body.

set shot: *Basketball:* A normally two-handed shot taken from a "set" or stationary position at a distance of 20 feet or more. The set shot is seldom used in modern basketball.

setter: *Volleyball:* The player who puts the ball in position so it can be spiked by a teammate.

setup: A potentially easy victory.

seventh-inning stretch: A custom followed by spectators at baseball games in which they stand and stretch. Hometown fans stretch before the beginning of the seventh inning; fans of the opposing team, before the beginning of the second half of the inning.

shadow: *Ice Hockey:* A player assigned to closely guard a particular opponent.

shadow bowling: Practicing without any pins set up.

shaft: *Archery:* The main part of the arrow.

shake off: *Baseball:* To reject — on the part of the pitcher — a signal given by the catcher; so-called because the pitcher often shakes his head.

shank: *Golf:* To hit the ball, not with the face of the clubhead, but with the heel, causing a poor shot. *Football:* To kick the ball with the side of the foot, causing it to veer sharply to the right or left.

sheet: *Sailing:* Any rope used to adjust a sail.

shell: *Rowing:* A long, light, narrow racing boat that is propelled by oarsmen. *Hunting:* A tube-shaped metal, plastic, or cardboard case that holds a charge of powder and shotgun pellets; a cartridge.

shift: *Football:* A change of position by one or more offensive players as they await the snap of the ball. *Ice Hockey:* The amount of time a particular player or line is on the ice.

shinguard: A protective covering, usually made of plastic, that covers the shin. Worn in goal games and by the catcher in baseball.

shoestring catch: *Baseball, Softball:* A catch made just before the ball hits the ground.

shoot: To discharge a gun or release an arrow toward a target; also, to drive a ball or puck toward the goal by throwing or batting it.

short: *Baseball, Softball:* Abbreviated term for shortstop.

short course: *Swimming:* A course at least 25 yards in length, but not more than 50 yards.

short fielder: *Softball:* A tenth player who is stationed between the infielders and outfielders.

short game: *Golf:* That portion of one's game that includes putting and approach shots.

shorthanded: *Ice Hockey:* To have fewer players on the ice than the opposition. A team becomes shorthanded when one or more of its players are sent to the penalty box for rule infractions.

short relief man: *Baseball:* A relief pitcher who is normally brought into the game in its final innings, and thus pitches only a "short" distance.

shortstop: *Baseball, Softball:* The infielder who is assigned to play to the left of second base and who is responsible, with the second baseman, for covering second base.

shot: *Track and Field:* The solid metal ball approximately five inches in diameter that is thrown in shot-put competition. In high school, boys hurl a 12-pound shot. In college competition, the shot weighs 16 pounds. *Hunting:* Small metal pellets used as ammunition in a shotgun.

shotgun: *Hunting:* A gun used for firing cartridges filled with small shot. *Football:* A primarily passing formation in which the quarterback is positioned several yards behind the center. Other backs and the receivers spread out to the right and left, ready to break downfield.

shotmaker: A good shooter.

shot put: *Track and Field:* An athletic event in which contestants attempt to throw a shot as far as possible.

shovel pass: A short, two-handed, underhand pass.

show: *Horse Racing:* To finish third.

showboat: A player who shows off; a hotdog.

shuffleboard: A game played on a long narrow court in which disks are slid along the smooth court surface toward a triangular-shaped scoring area using a long-handled implement with a pronged end.

shutout: A contest in which the losing player or team fails to score.

shuttle, shuttlecock: *Badminton:* A small rounded piece of cork or plastic with a crown of feathers that is batted back and forth across the net. Also called a bird.

side: One or two opposing groups or teams.

sidearm delivery: *Baseball:* A pitcher's throw made by sweeping the arm forward between shoulder and hip height.

sideline: The boundary line that determines a side of a playing field or court.

sideslip: *Skiing:* To position the skis across the slope and then to slide sideways downhill, controlling the rate of slide by edging.

sidespin: Spin imparted to a ball that causes it to rotate from side to side.

sidestep: *Skiing:* To ascend a slope with the skis across the slope. The uphill ski is placed down and firmly edged, and then the downhill ski is brought up to it.

sidestroke: *Swimming:* A stroke in which the swimmer is on one side and thrusts the arms forward alternately while executing a scissors kick.

sidesurfing: *In-line Skating:* A maneuver in which the skater glides with the heels of the skates facing one another, feet wide apart, and arms extended.

sight: A device for aiming a bow, rifle, or pistol.

sign: A signal by which a player or coach instructs members of his team as to a specific play or strategy. In baseball, a catcher uses his fingers to give the pitcher a sign for a certain pitch. A baseball coach gives a sign to a base runner telling him to steal. A football coach gives a sign to the defensive team, instructing the players to use a certain alignment.

signal caller: *Football:* The quarterback.

signals: *Football:* The words used by the quarterback in the huddle to inform the other players as to the formation and play to be used on the upcoming down. The quarterback also uses signals at the line of scrimmage to instruct the center when to snap the ball.

silks: *Horse Racing:* The distinctly colored and patterned jackets and caps worn by jockeys or harness drivers to identify the owner of the horse.

silver medal: In the Olympic Games and other sports competition, the silver or silver-colored medal awarded for a second-place finish.

sin bin: *Ice Hockey:* See penalty box.

single: *Baseball, Softball:* A base hit in which the batter reaches first base.

singles: *Badminton, Tennis, Table Tennis:* A match between two players.

sink: *Golf:* To putt the ball into the hole.

sinker: *Baseball:* A pitch that drops groundward as it nears the plate. *Fishing:* A lead weight attached to the line to hold it and the bait or lure underwater.

sit spin: *Figure Skating:* A spin on one skate in which the skater sinks to a sitting position.

sit-up: An exercise performed by first lying on the back, and then raising the body to a sitting position, with the knees slightly bent.

sitzmark: *Skiing:* The depression one makes in the snow by falling backwards and sitting down.

sixth man: *Basketball:* The player who is regularly used as the team's first substitute.

skate: A metal blade attached to the sole of a boot that is used in gliding over the ice. Also, a roller skate.

skateboard: A short, narrow board, one and a half to two feet in length, equipped with two pairs of small wheels, one pair at each end.

skate guard: A device that fits over the blades of an ice skate to protect the blade edges when the skate is not in use.

skating: Gliding or moving along the ice on skates.

skating foot; skating leg: *Figure Skating:* The foot or leg that supports the body's weight when the skater is on one foot; opposed to the free foot or leg.

skeet shooting: The sport of shooting at clay targets thrown from traps.

ski: A long, narrow, flat runner of wood, metal, or other material that curves upward in the front. Worn in pairs, skis are attached to the soles of special boots for gliding or traveling over the snow.

ski boot: A heavy, thick-soled boot which encloses the ankle, and to which the binding is attached that fastens the boot to the ski.

skiing: The sport of gliding or traveling on skis.

ski jumping: A sport in which the skier jumps for distance after skiing down a long sloping course.

ski lift: Any of the various power-driven devices used to carry skiers to the top of a slope. Towing bars, suspended chairs, and gondolas are types of ski lifts.

skimobile: See snowmobile.

skin diving: Underwater swimming in which the diver is equipped with a snorkel, swim fins, and a face mask.

ski patrol: Members of a volunteer organization, all expert skiers, who help injured skiers by administering first-aid and assisting them from the slopes.

ski pole: A long, slender, tapered pole with a point at one end and a hand grip at the other, used in pairs to assist the skier in climbing, walking, and turning.

skipper: The captain of a boat; also, the manager of a baseball team.

ski touring: See cross-country skiing.

skittles: A bowling game in which a wooden disk or ball is thrown to knock down nine pins set up in a diamond-shaped arrangement.

ski wax: Special wax applied to the running surface of skis to vary their slipperiness, depending on snow conditions.

sky diving: The sport of jumping from an airplane and performing various stunts before pulling the ripcord of a parachute. Also called sport parachuting.

slab: *Baseball:* The pitcher's rubber. See rubber.

slalom: A race along a zigzag course laid out with flag-topped poles called gates. Slalom racing used to apply only to downhill skiing, but it has been adopted by water skiers and motor sports enthusiasts.

slam dunk: *Basketball:* A dunk shot of unusual force.

slant: *Football:* A running play in which the ball-carrier moves into the line at an angle.

slap shot: *Ice Hockey:* A hard shot made by bringing the stick into a high backswing, then forward, hitting the ice and puck simultaneously, causing the puck to be lifted from the ice.

slashing: *Ice Hockey:* Swinging a stick at an opponent. A penalty is given for slashing.

sleeper: *Bowling:* A pin hidden behind another pin.

slice: *Golf:* A ball hit by a right-handed player that curves off the course to the right. *Tennis:*

A stroke hit with backspin; also, a stroke hit with underspin.

slide: *Baseball, Softball:* To drop to the ground and skid, usually feet first, into a base to avoid being tagged out.

slider: *Baseball:* A breaking pitch thrown like a fastball and, in its early stages, with the appearance of a fastball, but that breaks in the same direction as a curve.

slip: *Boxing:* To avoid a blow by moving the head.

slot: *Football:* On the offensive line, a wide gap between a pass receiver and a tackle.

slotback, slotman: *Football:* A back or pass receiver who lines up behind the slot.

slow pitch softball: A type of softball in which pitches must be delivered at moderate speed and travel in an arc between three to 10 feet in height. There are 10 players on a team. Bunting and base stealing are not permitted.

slugger: *Baseball, Softball:* A long-ball hitter.

slugging average: *Baseball:* A statistic meant to indicate a batter's effectiveness in making extra-base hits. It is determined by dividing the times at bat into the total bases. Thus, a player with 348 total bases in 574 times at bat would have a slugging average of .606.

slump: A period of time in which a player or team lacks in effectiveness.

smash: In tennis and other racket sports, a hard overhead stroke.

smoke: *Baseball:* A fastball.

snap: *Football:* The action of the center in putting the ball in play by handing or passing it between his legs to the quarterback, punter, or holder.

snatch: *Weight Lifting:* A lift in which the weight is raised in a single motion from the floor to a position directly overhead with the arms fully extended.

snooker: A game played on a special six-pocket, cloth-covered table, resembling the table used in pocket billiards, with 15 red and six nonred object balls and one white cue ball.

snorkel: A rubber or plastic often J-shaped tube held in the mouth and used for breathing by a skin diver.

snowmobile: A small motorized vehicle with ski-like runners in front and tank-like treads in the rear, used for traveling over the snow.

snowplow: *Skiing:* A method of slowing or stopping in which the tips of the skis are brought close together, causing a "plow" effect.

snowplow turn: *Skiing:* A turn made from a snowplow position.

snowshoe: A lightweight, racket-shaped frame strung with leather strips that can be attached to the foot to permit walking on deep snow.

soccer: An international game played by two teams of 11 players each on a rectangular field with net goals at each end. The object is to drive a round inflated ball past the opposing goalkeeper into the goal for a score. The ball is moved mainly by kicking. The hands and arms cannot be used.

softball: A game similar to baseball that is played on a smaller diamond, the bases 60 feet apart, with a larger ball that is pitched underhand. A softball game lasts seven innings.

sour apple: *Bowling:* A split in which the 5, 7, and 10 pins are left standing.

southpaw: A left-hander; the term is common to baseball in referring to a left-handed pitcher, but it also applies to a boxer who leads with his right hand.

span: The distance between the thumb hole and finger holes over the surface of a bowling ball.

spar: To box, usually in a practice session. *Sailing:* Any stout metal or wooden pole used to support or extend the sails.

spare: *Bowling:* The knocking down of all 10 pins with two successive rolls of the ball.

sparring partner: An individual hired to spar with a boxer in training for a bout.

spear: *Football:* To lunge helmet-first at an opponent. *Ice Hockey:* To jab an opponent with the stick blade; illegal.

spearfishing: The sport of stalking fish with a spear gun in skin diving.

spear gun: A gun that shoots sharp-pointed, barbed spears used in spearfishing.

special team: *Football:* One of several squads of players used by a team on punts, field-goal attempts, kickoffs, and in returning punts and kickoffs. Because most players are running at full speed on these plays, the special-team injury rate is higher than normal. Also called bomb squad, suicide squad.

speed bag: *Boxing:* A lightweight, teardrop-shaped punching bag used to develop speed and timing.

speedboat: A fast motorboat.

speed skate: A long, flat-bladed skate in which the blade ends project beyond the ends of the boot. The long blades enable the skater to achieve the utmost speed.

speed skating: The sport of racing on skates.

spike: The sharp metal plate or nail-like projection fixed to the sole of a shoe for traction. Spikes are worn in such sports as baseball, softball, golf, and some track and field events. *Baseball, Softball:* To cut or otherwise injure a player with one's spikes. *Football:* To slam the ball to the ground in the end zone after scoring a touchdown. *Volleyball:* To drive the ball down hard at a sharp angle into the opponent's court so that it cannot be returned.

spinning reel: *Fishing:* A reel that permits the line to unwind with the pull of the lure that is cast.

spinning rod: *Fishing:* A relatively flexible rod for holding the spinning reel; its ring guides are large enough to permit the line to unwind freely.

spiral: *Football:* The rotation of the ball on its long axis after it has been passed or punted. *Skating:* A body position in which the skater bends forward, one leg extended backward with a straight knee, the arms extended out to the side.

spitball, spitter: *Baseball:* An illegal pitch in which the ball or fingers are moistened with spit, Vaseline, or other foreign substance.

splice: *Bowling:* The area where the alley's maple boards are joined to the pine boards.

split: *Bowling:* An arrangement of pins that occurs after the first ball of a frame has been delivered in which two or more pins are standing with one or more pins down between them. *Gymnastics, Figure Skating:* A position in which the legs are stretched out at right angles to the upper body.

split decision: *Boxing:* A decision awarded a boxer by most but not all of the official judges.

split end: *Football:* A pass receiver that lines up several yards away from the player closest to him.

split finger fastball: *Baseball:* A pitch that is gripped between the forefinger and middle finger and thrown straight overhand. It drops as it nears the plate, breaking to the right or left.

splits: *Track:* The recorded times of a distance runner at various intervals, as at every eighth of a mile in a mile race.

splitter: See split finger fastball.

sport: A pastime or recreation, usually involving physical exercise, and having a formal set of rules.

sport parachuting: See sky diving.

spot: To grant a certain number of points to an opponent as a handicap. A superior table tennis player might spot an opponent five points. *Bowling:* Any one of the small dots or triangles embedded in the lane at a distance of from 12 to 16 feet from the foul line, used by bowlers in targeting the ball. *Pool, Billiards:* Any one of the three small round spots on the table used in placing object balls, usually after a foul.

spot bowling: A method of bowling using the dowels or rangefinders as targets in aiming for the pins.

spotter: A person who assists a television or radio broadcaster by identifying the players on the field. *Gymnastics:* An instructor who assists by supporting, lifting, or catching the gymnasts as a stunt is being performed during a practice session.

spray hitter: *Baseball:* A hitter who drives the ball to all fields.

spread: See point spread.

springboard: *Diving:* A strong, flexible board, 16 feet long and 20 inches wide, used to spring the diver into the air.

spring training: *Baseball:* A period beginning in late February or early March and extending to the opening day of the season, used by professional teams for conditioning and practicing and for exhibition games.

sprint: *Track:* A race run at top speed from beginning to end. Sprints are commonly run at distances of 50, 60, 100, 220, 300, and 440 yards, and 100, 200, and 400 meters. Also called a dash.

square-in: *Football:* A pass route in which the receiver runs downfield for several yards, then cuts at a right angle toward the center of the field.

square-out: *Football:* A pass route in which the receiver runs downfield for several yards, then cuts at a right angle toward the nearest sideline.

squash: See squash racquets.

squash racquets: A game played on a four-walled court with a racquet and small rubber ball. Sometimes called squash.

squash tennis: A game similar to squash racquets but played with a larger, harder ball and a larger, heavier racquet.

squeeze, squeeze play: *Baseball:* A play in which a runner on third base breaks for home plate as the pitch is delivered. He depends on the batter to bunt the ball so he can score.

staggered start: *Track:* A start of a race in which contestants are assigned starting points that serve to compensate for the unequal distances each is to run. Runners in the outside lanes start farther ahead than those in the inside lanes.

stag position: *Gymnastics, Skating:* A body position during a leap in which one's legs are spread, but with the front leg bent so the foot is held beneath the body.

standardbred: One of an American breed of horses developed for harness racing.

standing broad jump: *Track and Field:* A jump made for distance without a running start.

Stanley Cup: The trophy awarded to the winner of the championship playoffs of the National Hockey League.

starboard: *Boating:* The right side of a boat when one is facing forward.

starting block: *Track:* A device against which the runner braces his feet at the start of a short race.

starting pitcher: *Baseball:* The pitcher named to start a game for a team. He must pitch until he retires the first batter or the batter reaches first base.

steal: *Baseball, Softball:* To run for a base and reach it or attempt to reach it before an opposing player can throw the ball there.

steeplechase: *Horse Racing:* A race across open country or over a course with such obstacles as fences and water jumps. *Track:* A race in which competitors must clear hurdles and a water jump.

steer roping: *Rodeo:* An event in which a mounted cowboy must rope a full-grown steer, jerking the animal to the ground, then dismounting and tying any three legs of the animal.

stem: *Skiing:* To slide the tails of a ski outward and edge it usually before making a turn.

stern: The rear part of a boat.

stickball: A form of baseball played on city streets with a small rubber ball and the handle of a broom for a bat.

stick check: *Ice Hockey:* To use one's stick to hit, hook, or sweep the puck away from an opposing player.

stickhandle: *Ice Hockey:* To carry the puck along the ice with one's stick.

stirrup: The flat-bottomed loop or ring hung from either side of a horse's saddle to support the rider's feet.

stock car: A racing car that looks like an ordinary passenger car, but that has been torn apart and rebuilt from the ground up to create power and speed.

stopper: *Baseball:* A pitcher who can be relied upon to end a team's losing streak.

straddle position: *Gymnastics:* A body position in which the legs are spread wide apart.

straddle, straddle roll: In high jumping, a technique in which the jumper crosses the bar belly down, one leg leading the jump, the other trailing.

straight arm: *Football:* To ward off a tackler by using one's hand and arm.

straight pool: A pocket billiards game in which each player must call the ball he intends to sink and designate the pocket in which he intends to sink it. Each ball pocketed is worth one point. The first player to score an agreed upon number of points — 50, 100, 125, or 150 — wins the game. Also called 14.1 Continuous.

straight rail billiards: A billiards game in which a point is scored each time the cue ball rebounds from one of the object balls to the other.

strand: *Baseball, Softball:* To leave one or more runners on base.

strangle hold: *Wrestling:* Any hold used to choke an opponent; illegal.

streak: A series of consecutive wins or losses.

stretch: *Horse Racing, Track:* The last stage of a race; the homestretch. *Baseball:* The arm action a pitcher uses when there is a runner on base in which he raises both hands to about head height, then checks the position of the runner before beginning his delivery.

strike: *Baseball, Softball:* A pitched ball that is swung on and missed or one judged to have been in the strike zone. A pitch hit foul is also a strike. The batter is out after three strikes have been called against him. *Bowling:* The act of knocking down all the pins with the first roll of the ball. *Fishing:* The sharp pull on the line when the fish takes the bait or lure.

strike out: *Bowling:* To finish a game with three strikes in the 10th frame.

strikeout: *Baseball, Softball:* The out that results after a batter has been charged with three strikes.

striker: *Soccer:* Any of the team's forwards.

strike zone: *Baseball, Softball:* The area over home plate that is generally between the level of the batter's knees and shoulders through which the ball must pass in order to be judged a strike.

string: *Bowling:* A complete game; 10 frames.

stroke play: *Golf:* Competition in which the winning player or side is determined by the total number of strokes to complete the round. The side taking the fewest strokes wins. Also called medal play. See match play.

strong side: *Football:* The side of an unbalanced line with the larger number of players.

stuff, stuff shot: *Basketball:* See dunk shot.

stunt: *Gymnastics:* Any exercise included in a routine.

stutter step: *Football:* A series of quick, short steps taken by the ballcarrier in an effort to elude a would-be tackler.

stymie: *Golf:* A situation in which an opponent's ball lies directly in the path of the ball to be putted. The ball causing the stymie must be picked up, its position first being marked.

substitute: A player who enters a game in place of another.

sudden death: An overtime period in which the team that scores first wins the game.

suicide squad: See special team.

sulky: *Harness Racing:* The light, two-wheeled vehicle that is drawn by the horse.

Super Bowl: The championship game of the National Football League that matches the American Conference champion and the National Conference champion.

superstar: A professional athlete who has attained unusual stature by virtue of his exceptional ability, his popularity with the fans, his huge earnings, and the media coverage he receives.

surfboard: The narrow, lightweight, somewhat rounded board used by surfers for riding waves in to shore.

surfcasting: The sport of fishing from shore; casting one's line into the surf.

surfing: A sport in which one paddles a surfboard out into the surf, then, standing on the board, attempts to ride a wave back to shore.

surfer: An individual who takes part in surfing.

swan dive: *Diving:* A dive performed with the legs straight, the back arched, and the arms stretched out to the sides.

sweat suit: A two-piece cotton-jersey outfit consisting of a long-sleeve shirt and long pants, tightly fitted at the ankles and waist, often worn during a warm-up period or practice session.

sweep: *Football:* A play in which the ballcarrier dashes for the outside behind blocking linemen before turning upfield.

sweep check: *Ice Hockey:* An attempt to get the puck from an opponent by putting one's stick nearly flat to the ice and sweeping the blade toward the puck.

sweeper: *Bowling:* A ball that strikes the 1-3 pocket, then sweeps the pins into the pit. Also called a broom ball.

sweet spot: The spot toward the end of a baseball bat, on the face of a golf club, or at the center of a paddle or racquet on which the ball is best hit.

swim fin: A runner or plastic foot covering with a wide, flat, flexible front portion that is worn in pairs and used to give added thrust to a diver's kicks. Also called a fin or flipper.

swimming: Propelling oneself through the water by means of leg kicks and arm strokes. Swimming races are held at many different distances and involve four different strokes: the backstroke, breast stroke, butterfly, and crawl.

swing pass: *Football:* A short pass to a back running to the outside.

switch: *Basketball:* A defensive maneuver in which one player exchanges defensive responsibilities with a teammate, guarding an offensive man to whom he is not normally assigned.

switchback: *Auto Racing:* A hairpin turn, sometimes found on mountain race courses.

switch-hitter: *Baseball, Softball:* A batter who is capable of batting either right-handed or left-handed.

T

table tennis: A game similar to tennis that is played on a rectangular table nine feet long and five feet wide. Players with rubber-faced paddles hit a small plastic ball back and forth across a six-inch-high net.

tachometer: *Auto Racing:* An instrument that measures the engine's speed in terms of revolutions per minute. Also called a rev counter.

tack: *Sailing:* To sail in a zigzag course against the wind.

tackle: The equipment used for such sports as fishing and archery. *Football:* The act of seizing the ballcarrier and throwing him to the ground or otherwise stopping his forward progress. Also, one of the two offensive linemen positioned on either side of the center between the guard and the end. *Soccer:* To use one's feet to take the ball from an opponent.

tag: *Baseball, Softball:* To put a runner out by touching him with the ball or with a gloved hand that holds the ball.

tag up: *Baseball, Softball:* To remain touching a base when a ball is hit with the idea of advancing to the next base after the ball is caught. A runner normally tags up after a sacrifice fly. See sacrifice fly.

tail: The rear part of a ski.

take: *Baseball, Softball:* To let a pitched ball go by without swinging at it.

tap: *Bowling:* The instance of having a single pin remain standing after what was apparently a perfect hit.

tape: In tennis and other net games, the narrow strip of woven fabric that runs along the top of the net. In track and field events, the tape is the string or yarn that is stretched across the finish line of a race course to be broken by the winner.

tap-in: *Basketball:* A shot made by tapping a rebound toward the basket.

tap-off: *Basketball:* See tip-off.

target: A usually circular object that is marked with circles to be used in rifle, revolver, or archery practice.

target archery: Competitive archery in which individuals take turns shooting groups of arrows at round targets over various distances.

Tartan Turf: A carpet-like synthetic surface used in place of grass.

T-bar: *Skiing:* A lift that consists of a T-shaped bar that is suspended from a moving overhead cable. Skiers in pairs lean against the bar crosspiece to be pulled up the slope.

team: Two or more players that make a side in a game.

team foul: *Basketball:* A personal foul committed by a player and charged to the team as one of a specified number of fouls permitted before the bonus free-throw rule takes effect.

team tennis: Professional tennis played by teams of men and women. A match consists of five sets in these categories: men's singles, women's singles, men's doubles, women's doubles, and mixed doubles. Each set is won by the side winning six games, and a game is won by the side getting four points. The team that wins the match is the one that wins the most games.

technical foul: *Basketball:* An infraction by a player or coach that involves unsportsmanlike conduct. The penalty is one free throw awarded to the opposing team.

technical knockout: *Boxing:* A victory awarded by the referee when one boxer appears too badly beaten to continue.

tee: *Football:* The U-shaped plastic stand used to hold the football in an upright position for kickoffs. *Golf:* A small wooden or plastic peg upon which the ball is placed for the first stroke of a hole. Also, the area from which the golfer makes the first stroke of a hole.

tee off: *Golf:* To drive the ball off the tee at the start of play on a hole.

tennis: A singles or doubles game played on a rectangular court divided by a net by opposing players using racquets and a light, pressurized ball. The object of the game is to execute a stroke that lands within the court boundaries but that cannot be returned by the opposing side.

tennis elbow: *Tennis:* Soreness of the elbow believed to be caused by excessive or incorrect stroking.

tenpin: See bowling pin.

tenpins, tenpin bowling: A game in which one rolls a 12- to 16-pound ball down a 60-foot wooden alley in an attempt to knock down 10 pins, each approximately 15 inches in height and weighing more or less than three and a half pounds. A game is made up of 10 frames, each of which consists of two attempts to topple the pins. Players compete against one another or as members of a team.

10-second rule: *Basketball:* A rule that requires the offensive team to bring the ball across the mid-court line within 10 seconds after gaining possession of the ball in its backcourt.

Texas leaguer: *Baseball, Softball:* A fly ball that drops between an infielder and an outfielder for a hit.

T formation: *Football:* An offensive formation in which the quarterback lines up directly behind the center, and two or three running backs are positioned four or five yards behind the quarterback.

third base: *Baseball, Softball:* The base on the left side of the infield.

third baseman: *Baseball, Softball:* The infielder who is assigned to play to the right of third base, and is responsible for covering the base.

30-second rule: *Basketball:* A rule in women's basketball that requires the offensive team to try for a field goal within 30 seconds after gaining possession of the ball.

thoroughbred: One of a breed of horses developed and trained for racing.

three-cushion billiards: A billiards game in which the cue ball must strike three or more cushions as well as both object balls in order for a point to be scored.

three jump: *Figure Skating:* See waltz jump.

three-point play: *Basketball:* A play that results when a player who scores a field goal (two points) is fouled in the act of shooting. If the player is successful with the free throw that he is awarded, it results in a third point.

three-point stance: *Football:* A ready position assumed just before the play begins by linemen and running backs in which a player crouches with his feet spread, leaning forward to put the fingers or knuckles of one hand to the ground.

three-second rule: *Basketball:* A rule stating that a player cannot remain within the free throw lane for more than three consecutive seconds when his or her team is in possession of the ball.

three turn: *Figure Skating:* A turn on one skate from forward to backward (or backward to forward) from an outside edge to an inside edge (or from an inside edge to an outside edge).

throw: To propel an object through the air with a swift motion of the arm; to cast, to toss. *Pocket Billiards:* To cause an object ball to veer to the right or left as it heads for a pocket (by applying english to the cue ball). *Wrestling:* To force an opponent to the floor.

throw-in: In soccer and basketball, the method of putting the ball in play after a team has been awarded the ball out of bounds.

tie: A game or contest in which both sides have the same score.

tie ball: *Basketball:* See held ball.

tie breaker: *Tennis:* A system of scoring used to break a tie.

tight end: *Football:* A member of the offensive line with excellent blocking ability who is usually positioned to the right of the right tackle, and who is assigned to catch passes or block.

tiller: *Boating:* A handle used to turn the rudder of a boat.

timekeeper: The person who keeps track of time during a game.

time-out: A short interruption in the regular period of play during which the clock is stopped. During a time-out, players rest, plan strategy, or substitutions are made.

tip-in: *Basketball:* A field goal made by deflecting a rebound into the basket.

tip-off: *Basketball:* The jump ball that starts a period of play. Sometimes called a tap-off.

tip-up: *Fishing:* Any of several devices used in ice fishing that holds line and a baited hook and includes a signaling device to alert the fisherman when a fish is biting.

toe pick: One of the sharp teeth at the front of a figure-skate blade that is used to grip the ice in certain jumps and spins. Also called a pick.

topside: *Boating:* Up on the deck of a boat.

topspin: *Tennis:* Spin imparted by bringing the racquet face over the top of the ball, also called overspin.

total bases: *Baseball, Softball:* The sum of the bases that a batter reaches safely by his base hits. A single is equivalent to one base; a double to two bases; a triple, three; and a home run, four.

total chances: *Baseball, Softball:* The sum of a player's putouts, assists, and errors (used in determining a fielding average).

touch: *Fencing:* A hit. *Soccer:* The area just outside the sidelines.

touchback: *Football:* The act of touching the ball to the ground behind one's own goal line, the ball having been propelled over the goal by the opposition team. The ball is then put in play at the team's 20-yard line.

touchdown: *Football:* A play worth six points and accomplished by carrying the ball across the opponent's goal, by completing a forward pass to a teammate across the goal line, or by recovering a fumble in the end zone. Scoring a touchdown also earns a team the opportunity to try for a point after touchdown.

touché: *Fencing:* A term used to indicate that one's body had been touched by an opponent's foil.

touch football: A variation of football played on an improvised field with various numbers of players to a side and without protective equipment, in which touching is substituted for tackling.

tournament: A contest involving individuals or teams that compete in a series of elimination games. See elimination tournament, double elimination tournament, ladder tournament, round robin.

towline: The line from a boat to a water skier.

tracing: *Figure Skating:* The white mark etched upon the ice by the skate blade.

track: A usually oval course of dirt or cinders laid out for running or racing.

track and field: Athletic events performed on a running track and the field that it encloses. The running events usually include dashes of 110, 220, and 440 yards (or 100, 200, and 400 meters), distance races of 880 yards, one mile, and three miles (or 800 meters, 1500 meters, and five kilometers). There are also relay races at 440 yards and one mile (or 400 meters and 1500 meters). The field events include the high jump, long jump, triple jump, pole vault, and hammer, discus, and javelin throws.

track racing: *Cycling:* A race on a specially constructed high-banked oval track.

trailer: A player in ice hockey, basketball, and other goal games who follows behind the player who is in possession of the puck or ball to be in a position to receive a pass.

trainer: A member of the staff of a ball club who assists the club physician in the medical treatment of players. The trainer normally administers first-aid and treats minor inuries. In boxing, the trainer is more of a teacher and coach, being responsible for the conditioning and development of a boxer.

trampoline: A sheet of strong, taut canvas or webbed fabric that is attached with springs to a sturdy metal frame and is used for acrobatic tumbling.

trap: *Baseball, Softball:* The instance of a fielder catching the ball immediately after its first bounce. It may appear that the ball was caught on the fly, and thus an umpire's ruling is frequently necessary on such plays. *Soccer:* The act of bringing a moving ball under control by stopping or deflecting it. The feet, legs, waist, chest, or head can be used in trapping. *Golf:* See sand trap.

trap block: *Football:* A block in which a defensive lineman is allowed to penetrate through the offensive line to be suddenly blocked from an unexpected direction by an offensive player. Also called a mousetrap.

trapshooting: The sport of using a shotgun to shoot at clay pigeons hurled into the air from spring traps. See clay pigeon.

traveling: *Basketball:* Walking or running illegally while in possession of the ball. After two steps, a player with the ball must remain in position, keeping the pivot foot to the floor or dribbling.

traverse: *Skiing:* To descend a slope diagonally rather than straight downhill.

trial heat: See heat.

trim: *Sailing:* To adjust the sails so that they receive the wind properly.

triple: *Baseball, Softball:* A hit on which the batter reaches third base safely. *Bowling:* Three successive strikes in a game. Also called a turkey.

triple crown: *Baseball:* The achievement of leading one's league in batting average, runs batted in, and home runs in a season. *Horse Racing:* The achievement of a thoroughbred winning the three most important races for three-year-olds during a single year. They are: the Kentucky Derby, Preakness Stakes, and Belmont Stakes.

triple jump: *Track and Field:* An event in which each competitor jumps for distance from a running start, landing first on the take-off foot (a hop), then on the other foot (a step), and ending on both feet (a jump). Also called hop, step, and jump.

triple play: *Baseball, Softball:* A rare defensive play in which three players are put out, thus ending the inning.

triple steal: *Baseball, Softball:* For each of three base runners to steal a base on the same play.

troll: *Fishing:* To trail a baited line from behind a slowly moving boat.

trot: The gait of a trotting horse. See trotter.

trotter: *Harness Racing:* A standardbred whose gait is a trot, that is, a horse in which diagonal pairs of legs move forward together.

trudgeon: *Swimming:* A stroke executed in a prone position that combines the arm motion of the crawl with a scissors kick.

try-out: A test or trial to examine and evaluate the skills of a candidate for a team.

T-stop: In various types of skating, a method of stopping in which the blade or wheels of one skate are dragged at right angles behind the other skate.

tuck: In diving and gymnastics, a body position in which the knees are bent, the thighs are drawn to the chest, and the hands grip the knees.

tug-of-war: A contest of strength in which two teams pull on opposite ends of a rope, each trying to pull the other across a dividing line between them.

tumbling: A sport in which individuals perform such acrobatic feats as somersaults, handstands, headstands, twists, and rolls.

turkey: *Bowling:* See triple.

turn in: *Football:* A pass route in which the receiver runs downfield for a short distance, then turns toward the middle of the field.

turn out: *Football:* A pass route in which the receiver runs downfield for a short distance, then turns toward one of the sidelines.

turn over: In football, basketball, and other team sports, to lose possession of the ball through a mistake (as a fumble or intercepted pass) or an infraction of the rules (such as stepping out of bounds or traveling).

24-second rule: *Basketball:* A rule in professional basketball that requires the offensive team to try for a field goal within 24 seconds after gaining possession of the ball.

twin bill: *Baseball:* A doubleheader.

twist: In diving and gymnastics, a stunt that involves a vertical rotation of the body.

U

umpire: A person appointed to rule on plays in various sports. In major league baseball, four umpires are used in a game. The one positioned behind the plate to call balls and strikes is designated the umpire-in-chief. In football, the umpire is the official stationed in the defensive backfield who watches for illegal line play. In tennis, the umpire sits on a high seat at one end of the net and serves as the chief official of the match, announcing the score, and, with the assistance of the linesman, watching for faults. In badminton, platform tennis, and other net games, the umpire's duties are similar.

unbalanced line: *Football:* A formation in which there are more players on one side of the center than the other.

underdog: An individual or team expected to lose.

under grip: *Gymnastics:* See reverse grip.

underhand: A throw or a stroke that is executed with the hand below the level of the shoulder and the palm turned upward.

unearned run: *Baseball, Softball:* A run scored as the result of an error or passed ball, or one that scores after the defensive team has had an opportunity of making the third out of the inning. See earned run.

uneven parallel bars: *Gymnastics:* A pair of parallel wooden or metal bars, each about eight feet long, and upon which various swinging and balancing movements are performed in women's gymnastics. The higher of the two bars is placed about seven and a half feet above the floor; the lower bar is about five feet above the floor. The distance between the bars, as measured from one set of the supports to the other, can vary from 21 to 30 inches.

United States Figure Skating Association (USFSA): The governing body of amateur figure skating in the United States.

United States Olympic Committee (USOC): The governing body representing the United States in the events of the Olympic and Pan-American Games. The organization selects, equips, transports, feeds, and houses team members.

United States Soccer Football Association (USSFA): A federation of state soccer associations that provides the rules of play and promotes soccer in schools, colleges, and with local associations.

United States Tennis Association (USTA): A federation of local tennis clubs, educational institutions, recreation departments, camps, hotels, motels, and other groups interested in promoting tennis.

unsportsmanlike conduct: Discourteous or unfair conduct by an individual, such as fighting or using profanity or abusive language. In basketball, the penalty for unsportsmanlike conduct is a technical foul. In football, a team can be penalized 15 yards.

up and back: In tennis, badminton, platform tennis, and other net games, a strategy used in doubles competition in which one partner covers the net while the other plays the backcourt.

uppercut: *Boxing:* A short swinging blow directed upward, often to the opponent's chin.

uprights: *Football:* The vertical posts that support the crossbar in a goalpost.

upset: A game or contest in which the favorite is defeated.

utilityman: *Baseball, Softball:* A substitute player who is capable of playing each of several positions.

V

Vardon grip: *Golf:* A method of gripping the golf club in which the little finger of the right hand nestles between the forefinger and middle finger of the left hand. Also called the overlapping grip.

vault: *Gymnastics:* A leap over a vaulting horse or pommel horse performed with a running start and by using the hands to lift and support the body.

vaulting horse: *Gymnastics:* A piece of equipment in women's gymnastics that consists of an upholstered body about five feet long and one foot wide and with its top surface about three and a half feet above the floor. Gymnasts vault over it from the side.

Vince Lombardi Trophy: The championship trophy awarded to the winning Super Bowl team.

volley: In tennis, platform tennis, and paddle tennis, a stroke made by striking the ball before it hits the ground. In volleyball and badminton, a volley is the only legal stroke.

(Should the ball or shuttlecock touch the court, it results in the loss of a point.)

volleyball: A game played on a rectangular court between two teams of six players in which an inflated ball is hit back and forth across a high net. The object of the game is to ground the ball on the opponent's side of the net.

W

waggle: *Golf:* To move the clubhead back and forth with short, quick motions when addressing the ball.

waive: In various professional sports, for a club to give up its claim to a player.

walk: See base on balls.

walking: *Basketball:* See traveling.

waltz jump: *Figure Skating:* A jump in which the skater takes off from a forward outside edge, executes a half turn in the air, and lands on the back outside edge of the other foot. Also called a three jump.

warm-up: A period of exercise or practice before an athletic event.

warm-up pitch: *Baseball, Softball:* The practice pitches thrown at the start of an inning or when a relief pitcher enters the game.

warning track: *Baseball:* A dirt or crushed stone strip several yards wide between the outfield's outer edge and the outfield fence. The track serves to warn an outfielder who is running to make a catch that he is nearing the fence.

washout: *Bowling:* A split in which the 1, 2, and 10 pins, or the 1, 2, 4, and 10 pins are left standing.

water line: *Boating:* The line on the hull of a boat to which the water surface rises.

water polo: A water sport played in a rectangular pool between two teams, each of which tries to pass an inflated ball into the other's goal.

water-ski: To ski in the water while being towed by a boat.

water ski: One of a pair of wood or fiberglass strips about six inches wide, six feet long, slightly upturned at the front, that are used to water-ski.

weak side: *Football:* The side of an unbalanced line with the fewest number of players.

wedge: *Golf:* An iron with a very slanted face that is used on pitch shots, chip shots, and in blasting out of sand traps. See iron.

weigh-in: *Boxing, Wrestling:* An official weighing before a match to establish that the competitors' weights are within their particular weight class or division. *Horse Racing:* The official weighing of the jockey, his saddle, and related equipment after a race to establish that the jockey raced at or below his announced weight.

weight belt: *Scuba Diving:* A webbed belt worn by the diver that holds lead weights. The weights serve to counteract the body's natural buoyancy and permit the diver to descend and remain at a chosen depth.

weighting: *Skiing:* Shifting the body's weight to one ski or another in setting the edges to execute a turn or traverse.

weight lifting: A sport in which weights are lifted competitively, with the victory going to the individual who lifts the heaviest weight in a given class.

welterweight: *Boxing:* A boxer who weighs between 137 and 147 pounds.

Western roll: *Track and Field:* A method of high jumping in which the jumper crosses the bar on his side, the uppermost leg leading.

wet fly: *Fishing:* An artificial fly that is designed to be used below the surface of the water.

wet suit: In scuba diving, surfing, and water skiing, a suit of artificial rubber that fits closely to the body, but is made so as to trap a thin layer of water between the body and the suit's inner surface. Once warmed by the body's heat, the water acts to insulate the body from the cold water.

white flag: *Auto Racing:* A flag used to signal drivers that only one lap remains in a race.

whitewash: To hold an opponent scoreless; to shut out an opponent.

wicket: *Croquet:* Any of the small wire arches through which players must direct the ball.

Cricket: Either of two sets of three stumps that serve as the target for the bowler and are defended by the batsman.

wide receiver: *Football:* Either of two pass receivers, each of whom is positioned on an end of the line. Wide receivers are usually the fastest, most elusive members of the offensive team.

wild-card team: In professional football, basketball, and soccer, a team that qualifies for playoff competition by virtue of having the best record of all the teams within the conference that did not automatically qualify.

wild pitch: *Baseball, Softball:* A pitch far off target that the catcher cannot be expected to catch, and that enables a base runner to advance.

Wimbledon: A term that refers to the All-England Lawn Tennis Championships played annually since 1887 at the All-England Croquet and Lawn Tennis Club at Wimbledon, just outside London.

win: To achieve a victory over others in a contest.

wind up: *Baseball, Softball:* To swing back the arm and raise the front foot in preparation for delivering the pitch.

windward: *Boating:* The side toward the wind.

wing, winger, wingman: *Ice Hockey, Soccer:* Either of two forwards who play on the opposing ends of the forward line.

winner's circle: *Horse Racing:* An area near the finish line where the winning jockey and horse are brought to receive awards and be viewed by the spectators.

winning pitcher: *Baseball, Softball:* The pitcher on the winning team who is given credit for the victory. For a starting pitcher to be declared the winning pitcher, he must pitch at least five innings in baseball, four innings in softball. A relief pitcher can be declared the winning pitcher by coming into the game with his team trailing or the score tied, then completing a winning game. A relief pitcher can also become the winning pitcher should he leave the game after his team has taken the lead.

wishbone: *Football:* A variation of the T-formation that is common to college football in which the quarterback is given several options to each play: to run with the ball, to pass, or to lateral to one of the running backs. The name is derived from the wishbone-shaped placement of the backs.

Women's International Bowling Congress (WIBC): The supervisory body of women's bowling in North America.

wood: *Golf:* A club with a wooden head. Woods are numbered from one to five. The lower the number, the less the club face slants. The one and two woods are normally used for shots off the tee; the other woods are used for fairway shots.

World Cup: *Soccer:* A trophy symbolic of the world championship. World Cup competition is held every four years among the more than 130 members of the *Federation Internationale* *de Football Association,* the international governing body of soccer. Each nation is represented by the best of its professional players.

World Series: *Baseball:* The series of baseball games played each fall between the championship teams of the American League and National League. The term is also now applied to championship competition in an assortment of other sports.

World Team Tennis (WTT): An association of teams in professional tennis.

wrestling: A sport in which each of two opponents tries to throw or force the other to the ground.

wrist shot: *Ice Hockey:* A quick shot executed without taking any backswing, but simply by snapping the wrists forward.

X: *Bowling:* The symbol for a strike in scoring a game.

X-ring: *Rifle Shooting:* A small circle within the bull's-eye of certain targets that is used to break ties. When two or more shooters have the same score, the one with the most holes in the X-ring is declared the winner.

Y

yacht: A sailboat or powerboat that is used for pleasure cruising or racing.

Yamashita: *Gymnastics:* A vault that includes a handspring that is performed with the body bent at the waist.

yard: *Sailboating:* A long, tapering spar fixed at right angles to the mast and used for supporting a sail.

yaw: *Boating:* Side-to-side movement of the boat.

yellow card: *Soccer:* The yellow card, about the size of an ordinary playing card, that is shown by the referee to indicate that a player who has fouled is being cautioned.

yellow flag: *Auto Racing:* The solid yellow flag that is used to signal the drivers to be cautious and refrain from passing because of dangerous conditions on the track.

Z

Zamboni: The four-wheeled vehicle that is used to vacuum excess water from a field with an artificial surface before a contest is played; also the vehicle that is used in resurfacing an ice hockey rink. The Zamboni lays down a thin film of water that freezes to become the new surface.

zone defense: A defensive system common to basketball, ice hockey, and many other goal games in which each member of the team on defense is assigned to cover a certain area of the court or field. See man-to-man defense.